The Wine Danced

THE WINE DANCED

Angela Ashwin

eagle

Guildford, Surrey

British Library Cataloguing in Publication Data. A catalogue record for this book is available from the British Library.

Published by Eagle Publishing Ltd, PO Box 530, Guildford, Surrey GU2 4FH.

Prayers from *Common Worship: Services and Prayers for the Church of England* are copyright © The Archbishops' Council, 2000, and are reproduced by permission.
Prayers from *The Methodist Worship Book* are © 1999 Trustees for Methodist Church Purposes, and are reproduced by permission.
Prayers from *The Sunday Missal* are © 1984 William Collins & Co Ltd.
The texts of the *Sursum Corda, Sanctus, Benedictus Qui Venit and Te Deum Laudamus* are from *Praying Together*, © 1988 by the English Language Liturgical Commission (ELLC).
Unless otherwise stated, Biblical quotations are from *The Holy Bible, New Revised Standard Version*, Oxford University Press, © 1989.
(JB) denotes *The Jerusalem Bible* (London: Darton, Longman & Todd, 1966).
(RSV) denotes *The Revised Standard Version* (The British & Foreign Bible Society, 1971).
(NEB) denotes *The New English Bible* (Oxford University Press, 1970).

Typeset by Eagle Publishing
Printed by Cox & Wyman
ISBN No: 0 86347 472 1

FOR SIMON HOLDEN CR

Titles by the same author include:

Patterns not Padlocks
Patterns not Padlocks (cassette tape)
Wait and See
Wait and Trust
Woven into Prayer

CONTENTS

PREFACE

Many people have helped and encouraged me to produce this book over the last few years, and it is impossible to mention everybody.

Thanks are due to Sr Elizabeth CE, who first suggested that I might write some meditations on Eucharistic themes. I also owe a great deal to the many people who responded to my questionnaire about Christian Spirituality and Worship, and to several liturgists who have given me time to talk through issues concerning the way we pray our worship, especially the Eucharist.

Much of this book has been inspired by teaching I received in two courses of lectures: one by the late Michael Vasey at Cranmer Hall, Durham from 1996–7, and the other by Fr Kevin Seasoltz OSB, at St John's Seminary, Collegeville, Minnesota, USA during the first semester of 2000.

I am grateful to the artists who have contributed to this book with such sensitivity, and also to Anne Lepine, for the wisdom she has offered concerning prayer and Eucharistic worship from a Methodist and Anglican perspective. Finally, I must thank David Wavre of Eagle Publishing for his unfailing patience and support, and my friends and family, on whose love and understanding I depend more than they perhaps realise.

FOREWORD

In this book, Angela Ashwin gives us a glimpse of God's activity – of how God shares our life and uses his creation to transform it.

She has that rare gift of seeing the divine in the ordinary, and of understanding how we ordinary people pray. These meditations on the transforming power of the Eucharist use the stuff of daily life to explore what it is that God is giving to us, and how we might use the opportunity of worship to respond to what is offered. Out of each glimpse of 'the outskirts of his ways', Angela draws a thread which she offers us 'for weaving'. Her hope is that we will weave for ourselves a whole kaleido-scopic tapestry where the themes of the book and our everyday experience are drawn together.

Angela has a passion for making life and worship one. Her purpose is to make us strive less in our worship so that God can work in us more. So often worship, and even prayer, becomes such a performance. It becomes centred on us and what we can do rather than on God and what he is giving us. By focusing on the cup, she offers us as the central image of the book not a sub-stance but a receptacle, not something that we have created but something which receives and holds what God is giving.

As someone committed to our worshipping better, I hope that the directness and realism of these meditations will enrich many people's experience of Eucharistic worship, and help renew a sense of God's transforming love in the crucible of our lives.

David Stancliffe
Bishop of Salisbury
October 2001

PROLOGUE

On 20th July 1969, the American astronauts Neil Armstrong and Edwin Aldrin completed the final stages of a momentous journey, in the Apollo 11 space capsule, that would make them the first human beings to walk on the moon.

Before they went down the steps to the moon's surface, Edwin (also known as Buzz) took out some Communion bread and wine that had been given to him by his Presbyterian church at home. He placed the containers on a small shelf, and contacted ground control at Houston, Texas, inviting all who were listening to keep a moment of silence to contemplate the events of those few hours, and to give thanks, each in their own way. Then he read some words of Jesus from John 15: 'I am the vine, you are the branches . . .'

Buzz then poured the wine into the chalice. And because the gravity on the moon is significantly less than that on earth, the wine swirled and curled its way gracefully up the sides of the cup.

As these men looked at our planet earth, which was suspended in space like an exquisite jewel, *the wine danced!*

INTRODUCTION

The Eucharist (also called Holy Communion, Mass or The Lord's Supper) is an extraordinary gift and an equally extraordinary activity. Central and crucial in the life of Christians, it is the place where Jesus, our risen Lord, gives himself to us in bread and wine. It is also a form of service where church-goers gather together to say and do roughly the same things week by week, much to the bemusement of our non-Christian friends.

Many people find Eucharistic worship a rich source of inspiration and spiritual nourishment. Yet there is also a certain amount of frustration, among both clergy and lay people, because the Eucharist does not always fulfil its potential to touch our lives and change us. Some of us struggle to find connections between our personal prayer and our experience of church worship. Others are anxious because Christian worship, including the Eucharist, does not seem to speak to many people in our Western world, in spite of a widespread spiritual hunger. There are many different reasons for this, ranging from the ways in which worship is planned, prepared and led, to questions about the expectations, prayerfulness and attitudes of worshippers.

With all this in mind, I have spent the last few years researching into how Christian worship, especially the Eucharist, feeds and connects with our personal life and prayer. I am grateful for the insights and wisdom I have received from many congregations and clergy, and also from liturgical teachers and writers. As a fruit of this exploration I am offering this book of meditations, designed to deepen our understanding of the Eucharist, strengthen our commitment and delight in worship, and increase our openness to its transforming potentials. Some meditations are intimately prayerful in style, while others contain a mixture of teaching and reflections. I hope that, having spent some time praying with a short section, the reader will take something from that into the experience of worship

16

itself. Another hope is that the good things of the Eucharist will increasingly spill over into daily life and prayer.

Obviously not all church services are Eucharists, and a wide range of preaching services and Services of the Word make up an important part of Christian worship, especially in the Free Church and Anglican traditions. Christ gives himself to us in Word as well as in Sacrament, and some sections in this book could apply equally to non-Eucharistic worship. Nevertheless the main focus here is on Holy Communion.

During the Eucharist itself, our personal praying weaves in and out of the collective praise and prayer. Sometimes the two become inseparable, especially at places such as the Collects (prayers which gather together or 'collect' the prayers of the community) and the intercessions (which bring together the concerns of us all). Other great liturgical moments, such as, 'Glory be to God on high', and 'Holy, holy, holy', sweep us up into the flow of praise and worship of the angels in heaven, and remind us that our humdrum attempts to worship are taken up into something far greater than ourselves. In this book I have attempted to celebrate the fact of our belonging to the communion of saints, and to open some doors and windows into the Eucharistic liturgy, so that the dazzling radiance of God may pour into our hearts.

For those who lead worship, there is the inevitable tension between being responsible for holding a service together and wanting to pray the liturgy at the same time. The topics explored in this book may help to provide a focus for prayer, at least before a service. It could also be useful for clergy and worship leaders to reflect upon how the themes in this book are fleshed out in the design and style of Eucharistic celebrations. I am keen to learn from those engaged in leading worship, and would welcome a response, via the publishers of this book.

Worship is the place where God's desire for us meets our openness to him. We need to offer our best to God, so that the atmosphere, welcome, prayerfulness and content of services are

17

as good as possible. Each act of worship is an *epiphany*,[1] a revealing to us of God's glory, if we can take it. Our task is to set the scene, and to find the language, imagery and actions in which we can engage with God with our whole being, not just our brains.

If we give space and priority to prayer in the rest of our lives, we are more likely to approach the Eucharist with a loving attention and generosity of spirit, both as leaders of worship and as those who are led. Conversely, the Eucharist is more likely to form and nourish our inner lives at a deep level if we also pray at other times during the week. Hence this book!

How to use this book – some suggestions

Although the reader may wish to skim through the book in order to get an idea of its flavour and content, the meditations are primarily meant to be pondered slowly, so that each one has a chance to sink in and take root at a deep level. I would suggest that you choose a single section, allowing a few moments to quieten down, and then work in an unhurried way through the text. Ultimately the Holy Spirit is the One who teaches us to pray, so it is good to ask the Spirit for guidance.

At the end of each section there is *A Word for Weaving*, which is a short reminder of the meditation that can be brought to mind at any moment. This may make it easier to weave the themes of the book into everyday life and consciousness, and may also provide an *aide-mémoire* when coming to church.

You could pray with one or two meditations (three at the very outside) during any one week before going to a service of Holy Communion on the Sunday. If you go to Mass several times a week, or if you attend The Lord's Supper only every few weeks or months, you will, of course, need a different pattern.

When deciding which meditations to use, you could simply work through the book from start to finish, reflecting on Jesus' self-giving in Part 1, thinking about Jesus' agony and the pain of the world in Part 2, and then using the prayers of self-offering and the meditations about the Eucharistic liturgy in Parts 3 and 4. Or you could move around, especially if certain topics make sense in your present situation, or in particular seasons of the church's year. For example, Part 2 could be used in Lent and Holy Week, or during a difficult time in your life.

There is much to be said for going back to a meditation that especially moved or challenged you. This is not an attempt to recreate a good experience for its own sake, or to try and make things happen a second time. On the contrary, we need to strive *less* in our prayer and worship, so that God can work in us more. The purpose of repeating a meditation is to go back to the place where God was touching or speaking to us, so that we are available for him to take us more deeply into whatever he wants to give us. This, in turn, may help us to come to church more open and receptive to the gift of Eucharist itself.

Finally, this book could be used in groups, as a prayerful springboard for a parish worship team, or as a focus for a discussion or meditation group, especially if the participants also worship together regularly at the Eucharist.

An outline of the book
In each of the first three parts, the words 'Take this Cup' have a different context and meaning.

PART 1: 'TAKE THIS CUP OF MY BLOOD' – *the Cup of Life*
Here the words **'Take this Cup'** refer to the moment when Jesus gives the cup of wine to his disciples at the Last Supper. The meditations consider ways in which Christ pours himself out in love for us.

PART 2: 'TAKE THIS CUP AWAY FROM ME' – *the Cup of Suffering*
In this part the words **'Take this Cup'** have a different meaning, as Jesus prays in the Garden of Gethsemane and asks God his Father to take this cup of suffering away from him. The

material reflects upon the massive cost of Jesus' self-giving, and the implications of this for our own lives, especially when we face suffering ourselves.

PART 3: 'TAKE THIS CUP OF MY LIFE' – *the Cup of Openness*
The words 'Take this Cup' now have a third application, as our prayer of openness in response to God's great love for us: 'Take this cup of my life, O Lord.' The gift that we offer to God is our receptivity and willingness to let the Spirit of Jesus pervade our whole lives.

PART 4: THE SHAPE OF EUCHARISTIC WORSHIP
These meditations correspond to the broad outline of the Eucharistic liturgy as it has evolved from the early days of the church, and which is used in most mainstream churches today.[2]

A note about denominations

The fact that I am an Anglican committed to sacramental worship is inevitably reflected in my terminology and emphases, and in the quotations from *Common Worship: Services and Prayers for the Church of England* (2000). Yet the themes in this book reflect the wisdoms of many Christian traditions. So I hope that the meditations (which also draw on Methodist and Roman Catholic sources) will resonate with a much wider circle than Anglicans alone.

Although I make occasional references to our use of church buildings, the ideas that I am exploring are just as relevant to House Communions or celebrations in other contexts, such as open-air pilgrimages.

Wine rather than bread?

Several books about the Eucharist use the word 'bread' in their titles. This may be partly to do with the old custom in the Roman Catholic Church of having 'communion in one kind', whereby the people would only receive the bread. I have decided to redress the balance by using the word 'wine' in my title, because I believe that bread and wine are equally important as distinct and complementary symbols, and also because . . .

. . . the wine danced!

Wine dancing –
familiar, yet different,
expected, but surprising,
the same, though transformed.

Wine dancing –
reminder of agony, scourging and nails,
yet pledge of love's victory,
mercy unquenchable,
love undeniable,
hope uncontainable,
beauty untameable.

Wine dancing!

PART 1

'TAKE THIS CUP OF MY BLOOD'

The Cup of Life

Then he took a cup, and after giving thanks he gave it to them, saying, 'Drink from it, all of you; for this is my blood of the covenant, which is poured out for many for the forgiveness of sins.'
MATTHEW 26:27–8

1. THE VICTORY OF LOVE

And they prepared the Passover meal. When the hour came, Jesus took his place at the table, and the apostles with him.

LUKE 22:13B–14

Simplicity and majesty,
homeliness and wonder,
familiarity and strangeness,
intimacy and sorrow.

Jesus gives the game away:
'This is my body, broken for you.
This is my blood, shed for you.
I give myself up for you all.
I am drained to the last drop.
O my people,
nothing you do to me
can stop me loving you.'

The very moment
when evil appears to be winning
is transformed into the ultimate gift
of divine love,
poured out and dancing towards us.

A WORD FOR WEAVING
'Nothing can stop me loving you.'

2. THE DANCE OF LOVE

Then he poured water into a basin and began to wash the disciples' feet and to wipe them with the towel that was tied around him.

JOHN 13:5

It was as beautiful as it was shocking.

*Jesus, their Master and Lord,
kneeling to wash their feet,
and moving from one to the next
in a kind of slow dance,
a disconcerting glimpse
of the lengths to which the love of God will go
— too much for most of us to bear.*

*A symbolic action,
challenging all our pride and ambition
and teaching us how to love.*

*A new way of showing us
that each person is infinitely valued
and precious in God's sight.*

*An unequivocal statement
that you and I
are the ones intended
for this extraordinary gift of love.*

A solemn dance of freedom and humility,
leading inexorably to the tragedy of Calvary,
but ending in the whirling tempo
of the resurrection.

The glory of God is Jesus washing the disciples' feet.
ARCHBISHOP MICHAEL RAMSEY (1904–88)

A WORD FOR WEAVING:
'Love one another as I have loved you'.

3. COULD HE HAVE GIVEN MORE?

Jesus knew that his hour had come to depart from this world and go to the Father. Having loved his own who were in the world, he loved them to the end.

JOHN 13:1B–2

With the sharpened awareness and clarity of vision of one who knows that he has not long to live, Jesus has reached the final outpouring of himself.

There is no time to waste, since his betrayal is imminent.

He has already taken the towel and washed the feet of his friends.

And now, with a purposefulness and passion that take their breath away, he says, 'This is my body. This is my blood.'

And he gives himself away.

'If thou art satisfied, I am satisfied.
It is a joy, a bliss, an endless delight to me that ever I suffered the Passion for thee; and if I could suffer more, I would suffer more.'

WORDS OF JESUS TO JULIAN OF NORWICH IN
CHAPTER 22 OF *THE REVELATIONS OF DIVINE LOVE*
BY JULIAN OF NORWICH (C.1342–1413)

A WORD FOR WEAVING:
What more could he have done for us?

4. DEATH FREELY CHOSEN

'For this reason the Father loves me, because I lay down
my life in order to take it up again. No one takes it from
me, but I lay it down of my own accord.'
WORDS OF JESUS IN JOHN 10:17–18

The time has come for Jesus to die,
although the reality of death has long been part of his life.

He has faced hostile opposition from the start,
yet this has not deflected him from his way of being,
which is God's way of being
– which is self-giving love.

And now the momentum of fear, jealousy and hatred
is reaching its climax.

At the Last Supper Jesus looks death in the eye.

In the paradox of total acceptance
he freely chooses what is inevitable,
holding his destiny in his hands,
and handing over his life to the first disciples
– and to us.

He surrenders his life
even before it is taken from him.

And in bread and wine he entrusts to us,
from one generation to the next,
a means by which he can continue
to give himself to us.

A WORD FOR WEAVING:
'Freely I lay down my life.'

5. YOU IN ME, I IN YOU

It is no longer I who live, but it is Christ who lives in me.
ST PAUL IN GALATIANS 2:20

Jesus says to us:

> Take this cup.
> This is my blood, my very life,
>   shed for you.
> Abide in me and I in you.
>
> Will you let my life flow into yours,
> and yours into mine?
>
> Will you let me journey with you,
>   heal your wounds,
>   dissolve your guilt,
>   and make you into the persons
>   you were created to be?
>
> Will you let me pray in you
> to our beloved Abba, Father?
>
> Will you be my Body on earth?

In his *Confessions*, which describe his journey into Christian faith, St Augustine (354–430) prays:

> I heard your voice calling from on high, saying 'I am the food of full-grown men. Grow and you shall feed on me. But you shall not change me into your own substance, as

you do with the food of your body. Instead you shall be changed into me.'

Because you are children, God has sent the Spirit of his Son into our hearts, crying, 'Abba! Father!'

GALATIANS 4:6B

A WORD FOR WEAVING:
Christ in me; I in him.

6. UNCONTAINABLE GENEROSITY

He always loved those who were his own in the world.
When the time came for him to be glorified by you, his
heavenly Father, he showed the depth of his love.
EUCHARISTIC PRAYER IV, *THE SUNDAY MISSAL*

We cannot handle your generosity, Lord.

In some ways we would feel better
if your love were rationed out
according to our merits and deserving.

But you insist on loving us
even when we wound and reject you.
And you teach us to love both friends and enemies,
as you yourself did.

Such love is uncomfortable.

So we try to limit it,
convincing ourselves that we can earn your love
by good behaviour,
or by our attempts to make amends.

Or we try to squeeze your mercy into neat packages,
tidy schemes of payment for sin,
clinging to the 'eye for an eye' kind of justice.

But you continue to give yourself to us,
unreservedly.

By the sheer magnetism of your goodness
you attract our hearts and expand our vision,
challenging and disturbing us

– without menace or threat –
to think and live according to your way.

In the end
your unstoppable, unmanageable,
uncontrollable generosity
gets the better of us.

I pray that you may have the power to comprehend, with all the saints, what is the breadth and length and height and depth, and to know the love of Christ that surpasses knowledge, so that you may be filled with all the fullness of God.

EPHESIANS 3:18–19

A WORD FOR WEAVING:
The depth of his love!

7. HE NEEDS US

Christ Jesus, . . . though he was in the form of God, . . . emptied himself, taking the form of a slave, being born in human likeness. And being found in human form, he humbled himself and became obedient to the point of death – even death on a cross.

PHILIPPIANS 2:5–8

As he washes my feet
he leans his head on my shoulder.

As he trembles in the garden
he asks me to watch and pray with him.

As they hustle him to Calvary
he needs my back to help him carry the cross-beam.

When he has given up his spirit
he lets me carry him to a tomb.

What mystery is this,
the unfathomable humility
of our Christ?

Only God
could be so strong,
so vulnerable,
so free.

He depends on us still
to celebrate his gift of Eucharist.

He places himself in our hands
waiting patiently
for us to receive him into our hearts.

He has made himself need us.
What indiscretion, what trustfulness.
Good or ill-placed, that rests with us.
What hope, what firmness,
what tenacity, what indomitable hope
In us.
CHARLES PÉGUY (1873–1914)

A WORD FOR WEAVING:
What trust in us!

8. THE PASSOVER JOURNEY

Jesus said to them, 'I have eagerly desired to eat this Passover with you before I suffer.'

LUKE 22:15

The Passover festival is rich in imagery and spiritual significance, and Jesus clearly intends the Last Supper to be understood in Passover terms.

At Passover, the Jews celebrate their deliverance from slavery in Egypt.
Jesus now offers us a new kind of freedom, from the grip of guilt, selfishness and fear.

The Hebrew slaves had to walk through the wilderness to reach the Promised Land.
Jesus now calls us to a journey of faith into the unknown future with God.

God fed his people with manna in the desert.
Christ, the Bread of Life, who fed the five thousand by the Sea of Galilee, nourishes and sustains us today.

The Israelites had to trust God to lead them during those forty years; they had to resist the temptation to look back longingly at the attractive yet fatal security of their former life in Egypt. We too have to persevere in our pilgrimage of faith, depending on God rather than relying on the false securities of power, possessions or reputation.

From earliest times the Christian life has been called 'the Way' (Acts 19:9), and Jesus is himself the Way, the Truth and the Life. Our journey along his way involves risk, but also gives us

35

hope and inner freedom.

Each Eucharist is itself a kind of journey, in which we move a little further towards our goal of life with God.

> The exodus in me is marching again
> and I am caught in struggle and pain,
> fighting the demon of discouragement
> who tags along and haunts my heart.
>
> God of the wandering ones and my God,
> protect me from the Egypt of my own making.
> Pillar of Fire and Cloud of Light,
> assure me that I am not alone.

JOYCE RUPP

Christ, our paschal lamb, has been sacrificed. Let us, therefore, celebrate the festival, not with the old leaven, the leaven of malice and evil, but with the unleavened bread of sincerity and truth.

1 CORINTHIANS 5:7B–8 (RSV)

A WORD FOR WEAVING:
Into the unknown with God!

9. FROM DEATH TO LIFE

'Unless a grain of wheat falls into the earth and dies, it remains just a single grain; but if it dies, it bears much fruit.'

WORDS OF JESUS IN JOHN 12:24

Fruit of the field,
      harvested,
            ground,
                  baked,
      giving birth to fresh bread.

Fruit of the vine,
      plucked,
            pressed,
                  crushed,
      giving birth to new wine.

Fruit of Mary's womb,
      taken,
            crucified,
                  killed,
      giving birth to new life.

This is the 'Paschal' or Passover mystery,
the Easter movement from death to life,
from pain to hope,
and from anxiety to trust,
that lies at the heart of every Eucharist.

A WORD FOR WEAVING:
From death to new life!

10. HOLY FIRE

Then Moses went up on the mountain, and the cloud covered the mountain. The glory of the Lord settled on Mount Sinai, and the cloud covered it for six days. Now the appearance of the glory of the Lord was like a devouring fire on the top of the mountain.

EXODUS 24:15–16A,17A

Are we becoming casual about what is holy?

In the fourth century Gregory of Nyssa likened Christian worship to approaching the mystery of God on the holy mountain. Just as Moses entered the cloud and came close to the ineffable, divine glory, we too come near to the radiance of God which we cannot see or endure directly, but which is hidden in Christ's presence in our midst.

The divine presence will always defy our attempts to grasp it in words or categories. In the end we are not asked to understand, but only to receive the life of God into ourselves.

At the Eucharist, the simple experience of eating and drinking goes far deeper than efforts of mind or logical argument. We act out what we can never fully explain. Action, sign and symbol in worship open up our inmost being to the glory of our transcendent Lord.

And all of us, with unveiled faces, seeing the glory of the Lord as though reflected in a mirror, are being transformed into the same image from one degree of glory to another; for this comes from the Lord, the Spirit.

2 CORINTHIANS 3:18

Pour upon the poverty of our love . . .
the transforming fire of your presence.
HOLY COMMUNION, ORDER ONE,
COMMON WORSHIP

A WORD FOR WEAVING:
Fire of love, purify me!

11. BEYOND US

The cup of blessing that we bless, is it not a sharing in the blood of Christ? The bread that we break, is it not a sharing in the body of Christ?

1 CORINTHIANS 10:16

A mystery
that attracts us
but is always beyond our grasp.

A message of love
expressed in wine and bread
but defying definition.

A gift that we hold in our hands
but never possess,
because we discover
that we are the ones being held.

Lord, we are guests at your table.
We come, not as people who know,
but as those who are known;
not as people who have found the answer,
but as those who have been found by you.

O the depth of the riches and wisdom and knowledge of God! How unsearchable are his judgements and how inscrutable his ways!

ROMANS 11:33

A WORD FOR WEAVING:
When I seek you, Lord, I am found by you.

12. THE NEW COVENANT – GOD'S PROMISE

Then he took a cup, and after giving thanks he gave it to them, saying, 'Drink from it, all of you; for this is my blood of the (new) covenant, which is poured out for many for the forgiveness of sins.'

MATTHEW 26:27

The 'covenant' is a bond of love and commitment between God and his people.

God always keeps his side of the promise; he will be faithful and present to us, come what may. But we must choose whether or not to be faithful and present to him in return.

A key moment expressing God's covenant with the Israelites was on Mount Sinai during their forty years in the wilderness. Here Moses splashed the blood of animals over the altar and the assembly. Blood, which was a symbol of life, became a sign of God's unshakeable commitment to his people.

At the Last Supper, Jesus sees the startling power in the symbolism of the shedding of his own blood.

A new and even greater bond of love and forgiveness is about to be made, with his own life-blood poured out as its seal and pledge.

In this new covenant (or 'testament') Jesus keeps his part to the uttermost, and asks us if we are willing, in return, to be part of his mission of love for the world.

We may be lukewarm, and our love may falter.
Christ loves us fiercely, and will never falter.

Though we rejected your love,
you did not give us up
or cease to fashion our salvation.

You made a covenant to be our God . . .
and prepared the way for our redemption.

From the Thanksgiving, Holy Communion for Advent,
The Methodist Worship Book

A Word for Weaving
'This is my blood of the new covenant.'

13. THE VINE

'I am the vine, you are the branches. Those who abide in me and I in them bear much fruit, because apart from me you can do nothing.'

WORDS OF JESUS IN JOHN 15:5

The Vine:
symbol of Israel,
uprooted in Egypt
and replanted in the Promised Land.

The Vine:
symbol of Israel,
sometimes bearing good grapes,
and sometimes unfruitful,
or ravaged and destroyed.

The Vine:
symbol of Jesus
and his people the church,
each of us united to Jesus
and to one another,
with branches intertwining
and interrelated,
dependent on the one Source
for our life.

The Vine:
source of good wine,
symbol of well-being and peace,
shalom and celebration,
laughter, merriment and delight.

We give thanks to you, our Father,
for the holy vine of your child David,
which you have made known to us
through your child Jesus;
glory to you for evermore.

FROM TEXT WIDELY THOUGHT TO BE A EUCHARISTIC LITURGY
IN *THE DIDACHE* (LATE FIRST TO EARLY SECOND CENTURY)

A WORD FOR WEAVING:
'I am the vine, you are the branches.'

14. GOING TO OUR HEAD

*There was a wedding in Cana of Galilee, and the wine
ran out. Six stone water jars were standing there, and
Jesus said to the servants, 'Fill the jars with water.' When
the chief steward tasted the water that had become wine,
he said, 'Everyone else serves the good wine first, and
then the inferior wine. But you have kept the good wine
until now.'*

BASED ON JOHN 2:1–11

Typical God!

Six huge water-jars
– almost one hundred and eighty gallons of wine –
enough to last for months, years.

A gift overflowing,
like the divine love itself,
always lavished upon us in abundance,
like grain pressed down, shaken together and running over!

When we drink the rich wine of the kingdom,
we can let it go to our head as well as our heart.
In Jesus, the water of our lives
is transformed
into the wine of the boundless possibilities
of a love-affair with God.

Drink with hope this wine;
. . . as a result, you will be intoxicated with charity.

HILDEGARD OF BINGEN (1098–1179)

Whenever we willingly receive Jesus' life into our own,
the result is resurrection and new hope.
Every time we die to self-centredness
– we rise!

So we have every reason to dance and sing,
'Blood of Christ, inebriate me!'

> *Soul of Christ, sanctify me.*
> *Body of Christ, save me.*
> *Blood of Christ, inebriate me.*
> *Water from the side of Christ, wash me.*
> *Passion of Christ, strengthen me.*
> *O good Jesus, hear me;*
> *Within your wounds hide me,*
> *and never let me be separated from you.*

FROM THE FOURTEENTH CENTURY *ANIMA CHRISTI*
COMMONLY ATTRIBUTED TO ST IGNATIUS (1491–1556)

A WORD FOR WEAVING:
Blood of Christ, inebriate me!

15. JESUS' PRESENCE

'I am with you always, to the end of the age.'
WORDS OF JESUS IN MATTHEW 28:20B

Jesus is present to us
in the gathered community,
in the words of Scripture,
and now in bread and wine,
in a way that is neither magical nor mechanical,
but is beyond scientific analysis.

He is here for us,
whether or not we recognise him
or choose to receive him.

His presence in our midst is pure gift,
and he offers us his very self –
not as a commodity that we can control,
but as a person whom we may encounter.

O Christ,
you draw our humanity into yours.

Deepen our union with you;
form and transform our attitudes and lives,
making us into your Body in the world
– your real presence!

Help us to become Eucharist.

'As the Father has loved me, so I have loved you; abide in my love.'

WORDS OF JESUS IN JOHN 15:9

A WORD FOR WEAVING:
'I am with you always.'

16. JESUS' SACRIFICE

Therefore be imitators of God, as beloved children, and live in love, as Christ loved us and gave himself up for us, a fragrant offering and sacrifice to God.

EPHESIANS 5:1

For Christians, sacrifice is about *gift* and *generosity*, and the Eucharist puts us in touch with Jesus' sacrifice in a unique way:

– not as a repetition of Jesus' once-for-all self-offering;

– nor as a mere reminder of a sacrifice made 2,000 years ago;

– but as a gift through which Christ's generous love and very presence, are, in some mysterious way, made real for us now.

'Sacrifice' can be a difficult concept, and may feel like an outmoded symbol for life today. We are uneasy because ancient peoples used to sacrifice things to their gods, in the hope of cajoling or pacifying them. The animal or object sacrificed was often seen as a substitute for the worshippers, taking away their guilt and sin.

In Old Testament worship, various animal sacrifices were offered to God. These were seen as God's gift to his people, instituted on Mount Sinai, as a means of thanksgiving or as part of a corporate prayer for forgiveness and the restoration of the relationship between God and his people.

The sacrifice of Jesus on the cross transcends all these, and is certainly not a crude appeasement of an angry God.

It is an act of generosity *by God*, in Jesus.

To sacrifice means, literally, 'to do something holy' or 'to make holy'. Jesus' whole life was a 'making holy' of every situation, through his total generosity.

The greater a person's vision and good-will, the greater their vulnerability. This is what Jesus' sacrifice was about. The more he lived a life of unconditional love and challenged the meanness and pride of legalistic religion, the more his enemies were filled with jealousy and plotted to kill him.

Jesus' self-offering on the cross was the culmination of the unceasing giving of himself that had characterised his entire life.

His sacrifice of himself on the cross achieved what thousands of burnt offerings had failed to do, because it was his own life that he freely laid down for us. And his life is God's life, given and shared with us still, as he invites us to be part of his sacrificial love for the world.

> *He died for all so that those who live might live no longer for*
> *themselves, but for him who died and was raised for them.*
> 2 CORINTHIANS 5:15

Beloved Lord,
accept our sacrifice of praise and thanksgiving
in response to your great sacrifice for us.

Accept the offering of our lives,
and take us with you
on the way of self-giving love.

A WORD FOR WEAVING:
Love so amazing, so divine, demands my soul, my life, my all.

17. LINKS ACROSS TIME AND SPACE

*They devoted themselves to the apostles' teaching and fel-
lowship, to the breaking of bread and the prayers.*

ACTS 2:42

Since the earliest days of the church, the followers of Jesus have
come together for teaching and fellowship, to break bread and
share the cup, in a rich variety of places, cultures, styles and lan-
guages.

Each time we participate in the Eucharist, we are linked to the
continuous chain of Christians who have lived and prayed
down the ages, and from whose communities many of our
liturgies and patterns of worship have evolved.

The act of breaking bread and drinking wine in memory of
Jesus also connects us with a house-communion in a mud hut
in rural Africa, a choral Eucharist in a great British cathedral, a
Folk Mass among the poor of South America, a Lord's Supper
in a chapel on a remote Scottish isle, and a thousand other
celebrations.

It is the same Christ, offering us the same gifts, and we are part
of something incomparably greater than our own congregation:
the great community, the koinonia or fellowship of the Body of
Christ.

All the communions of a life-time are one communion.
All the communions of all men now living are one communion.
All the communions of all men, present, past and future, are one communion.

Teilhard de Chardin (1881–1955)

From age to age you gather a people to yourself,
so that from east to west
a perfect offering may be made
to the glory of your name.

Eucharistic Prayer III, *The Sunday Missal*

A Word for Weaving:
Though we are many, we are one Body.

18. A GLIMPSE OF HEAVEN

'Truly I tell you, I will never again drink of the fruit of the vine until that day when I drink it new in the kingdom of God.'

WORDS OF JESUS TO HIS DISCIPLES IN MARK 14:25

Whenever Jesus shared a meal with his followers,
they were given a glimpse of the 'kingdom' or 'reign' of God,
where each person is valued,
and kindness, generosity and mercy prevail.

The kingdom of God that Jesus proclaimed
is something that we also experience now,
although its final completion is yet to come.

Christ has conquered the powers of Satan,
yet the battle of good against evil still continues,
and we long for the fulfilment of Christ's work, beyond time,
when all darkness shall be filled with his light,
and we shall live in peace with one another.

The Eucharistic meal gives us its own glimpse of the kingdom,
both for our present situation
and as an anticipation of the messianic banquet:

On this mountain the Lord of hosts will make for all peoples a feast of rich food, a feast of well-aged wines. Then the Lord God will wipe away the tears from all faces.

ISAIAH 25:6A, 8A

In the Eucharist, past, present and future come together,
and eternity intersects with time:
– we recall what Jesus did in his earthly ministry,
– we rejoice in what is now,
– and we look forward to what is to come.

> *'Those who eat my flesh and drink my blood have eternal life, and I will raise them up on the last day'.*
>
> WORDS OF JESUS IN JOHN 6:54

This perspective of 'both here and not yet'
helps us to live fully in each present moment,
and also to face up to our dying:

> If there is a journey that will take us where we long to be
> my friend believe, though you cannot see,
> you have arrived, you are already home:
> for the best is here
> and the best is still to come.
>
> TOM McGUINNESS

A WORD FOR WEAVING:
Christ has died; Christ is risen; Christ will come again.

PART 2

'TAKE THIS CUP AWAY FROM ME'

The Cup of Suffering

Then he withdrew from them, about a stone's throw away, and knelt down and prayed. 'Father,' he said, 'if you are willing, take this cup away from me. Nevertheless, let your will be done, not mine.'

LUKE 22:41–2 (JB)

The two occasions on which Jesus says, 'Take this cup,' appear to be diametrically opposite.

At the Last Supper he says these words to the disciples when he gives them the cup of wine, his life-blood, poured out for us.

And in the Garden of Gethsemane on the Mount of Olives, he prays to his Father, 'Take this cup away from me,' in a desperate moment of shrinking from what is to come.

In the end, these two merge into one, because Jesus' agony and death become the place where love overcomes hate, and the cross of suffering is transformed into the source of new life and hope for the world.

> *Who would know Sinne, let him repair*
> *Unto Mount Olivet; there shall he see*
> *A man so wrung with pain, that all his hair,*
> *His skin, his garments bloudie be.*
> *Sinne is that presse and vice, which forceth pain*
> *To hunt his cruell food through ev'ry vein.*
>
> *Who knows not Love, let him assay*
> *And taste that juice, which on the crosse a pike*
> *Did set again abroach; then let him say*
> *If ever he did taste the like.*
> *Love is that liquor sweet and most divine*
> *Which my God feels as bloud; but I, as wine.*
> GEORGE HERBERT (1593–1633)

19. 'TAKE THIS CUP AWAY FROM ME'

Then he withdrew from them, about a stone's throw away, and knelt down and prayed. 'Father,' he said, 'if you are willing, take this cup away from me. Nevertheless, let your will be done, not mine.'

Then an angel appeared to him, coming from heaven to give him strength. In his anguish he prayed even more earnestly, and his sweat fell to the ground like great drops of blood.

LUKE 22:41–4 (JB)

Jesus
shaken to the core
by the fearful prospect
of what is being asked of him.

Jesus
pushed to the limit and beyond,
wrestling with his destiny,
as the forces of Satan
throw their whole weight at him.

Jesus
shuddering before the challenge,
and sweating blood
as he cries out for help
from the One he knows as 'Abba'.

Jesus
needing an angel to hold on to him,
and finding,
through this wilderness of unspeakable pain,
the strength and the way
to say Yes to this cup of suffering,
and Yes to the truth of who he is.

Love is that liquor sweet and most divine
Which my God feels as bloud; but I, as wine.

GEORGE HERBERT (1593–1633)

A WORD FOR WEAVING:
Abba, Father.

20. NO HOLDING BACK

He took with him Peter and the two sons of Zebedee, and
began to be grieved and agitated. Then he said to them,
'I am deeply grieved, even to death; remain here and stay
awake with me.' And going a little farther, he threw
himself on the ground and prayed, 'My Father, if it is
possible, let this cup pass from me; yet not what I want
but what you want.' He went away and prayed for the
third time, saying the same words.

MATTHEW 26:37–9, 44B.

In Gethsemane
Jesus does not hold back
from naming the horror
of what is to come.

He does not deny or repress his fear,
or try to hide it from God.

Three times
Jesus needs to work through his agonising struggle.

Even he
has to go back and back to God,
making, taking back,
and making again
his total surrender to the Father.

Because of this,
Jesus liberates us
to be completely honest with God ourselves.

Like him, we can tell God exactly what we feel and fear
as many times as we need to do so,
in the safe place that is prayer.

And Jesus gives us the strength
to go through and beyond our pain,
with him.

Lord Jesus,
I do not want this cup of suffering;
I have no strength to deal with it.

Take me through and beyond my No,
into your courage and wisdom,
so that I may face what has to be endured
and accept what has to be done.

Thank you for staying with me.

A WORD FOR WEAVING:
Jesus, I depend on you.

21. WHERE GOD PRESSES IN MOST KEENLY

O Lord, you are my God; you have been a refuge to the poor, a refuge to the needy in their distress, a shelter from the rainstorm and a shade from the heat.

ISAIAH 25:1A, 4

At the very point
where our misery is most acute
and our confidence most raw and shaken,
God is closest to us.

At the very moment
when we feel most alone,
    most afraid,
    most exhausted,
God is pressing in most keenly to help us –
as he was for Jesus.

For these are times
when we have nothing left of our own.
We can only throw ourselves utterly
on the mercy of God.

And the angel of God is close by to strengthen us,
as he was for Jesus,
helping us to hold on to our courage,
as the divine love
pours into our broken-open heart.

A WORD FOR WEAVING:
Out of the depths I cry to you, O Lord. – PSALM 130:1

22. JESUS BECOMES THE CUP

Emptying himself of all but love,
he was born of Mary,
shared our human nature
and died on the cross.
HOLY COMMUNION FOR CHRISTMAS AND EPIPHANY,
THE METHODIST WORSHIP BOOK

Jesus' self-abandonment to God in Gethsemane
is so complete
that he becomes one
with the suffering he embraces.

He courageously takes into himself
the destructive energies of creation,
breaking the vicious circle of hate and evil
through the unconquerable power
of the divine love.

His 'Yes' in Gethsemane
echoes the *fiat* of his mother before him:
'Let it be done to me according to your will.'

An angel was there both times.

And a sword pierced both their hearts.

A WORD FOR WEAVING:
He becomes the cup of suffering, for us.

23. UNSTOPPABLE POWER

Judas, procuring a band of soldiers, went to the garden with lanterns, torches and weapons. Then Jesus, knowing what was about to happen, came forward and said to them, 'Whom do you seek?' They answered, 'Jesus of Nazareth.' Jesus said to them, 'I am he.' When he said this, they drew back and fell to the ground.

BASED ON JOHN 18:3–6

They cannot stop him being king.

In the Garden of Gethsemane,
the mob who have come to get him
fall to the ground
when he steps forward and says, 'I am he'.

During those agonised hours of prayer,
Jesus has conquered the temptation to escape
or save himself by using his divine power.

And now his whole being is filled
with an extraordinary calm and strength.
He is so transparent to God
that his authority bowls them over.

In spite of themselves,
they cannot help but recognise
the majesty of the man,
even at the moment of his total vulnerability.

Behold the man!   Behold the King!

A Word for Weaving:
Behold the man!

24. JUDAS

When Judas, his betrayer, saw that Jesus was con-
demned, he repented and brought back the thirty pieces
of silver to the chief priests and the elders. He said, 'I
have sinned by betraying innocent blood.'

MATTHEW 27:3–4A

Judas – beloved of Jesus,
       chosen with the rest . . .

Is Jesus somehow sharing the weight of responsibility with Judas
       when he says, 'Do quickly what you have to do'?

Does Jesus receive the betraying kiss
       with a reproachful look?
       Or does he gaze sorrowfully
       upon the one whose guilt is so great,
       yet whom he still calls 'Friend'?

What depths of anguish will rack Judas
       once he realises what he has done,
       and sees that Jesus is not going
       to take the world by force?

'Woe to the one by whom the Son of Man is betrayed!' says
Jesus. 'It would have been better for him if he had not been
born.' This is surely a lament, not a condemnation. Jesus' heart
is breaking for Judas, for he knows the burden of guilt and
despair that the disciple will bear.

Judas' death is closer in time to Jesus' death
      than that of any other of the twelve.
      You could say they died together.

Only the unconquerable divine love
      could possibly be strong enough
      to penetrate the agony in Judas' heart

Only the unconquerable divine love
      can ever find those of us who are lost
      and feel destroyed by what we have done.

Lord God,
      whose compassion reaches beyond the heavens,
      and whose love bears and redeems the evil of this world,
      have mercy on us all.

A WORD FOR WEAVING:
Lord, have mercy upon us.

25. EVERY TIME SOMEONE CRIES IN PAIN

Even though I walk through the valley of the shadow of death, I fear no evil; for you are with me, your rod and your staff – they comfort me.

PSALM 23:4

Lord Jesus, you are present
every time someone cries out in pain or despair.

There is no darkness that you have not entered,
no depth of loneliness that you have not plumbed.
You are with us in our anguish,
because you know it from the inside.

    You are wounded in our wounds;

    you share our deep hurts;

    you weep in our tears.

In the Eucharist
you touch our brokenness with yours.
Always marked with the wounds of love,
you offer us the bread of your body, broken for us,
and the cup of your blood, willingly shed

The love he gives us is a love that has made itself vulnerable to all that hatred can do and has conquered hatred –The life he gives us is a life that has been through death and proved the stronger.

MARIA BOULDING

Can I discern seeds of hope even in the worst moments of my own suffering, in my own story? Have I been able to become more loving and sensitive to others because of what has happened? Have I grown through painful experiences rather than become embittered?

O Christ, by your grace, make my hurts
into places of your presence and transforming power.

Let my pain become a flame that burns with your love,
so that your healing energy may overflow
into others who are wounded or without hope.

A WORD FOR WEAVING:
I will fear no evil.

26. THE BROKENNESS OF THE WORLD

Why do the wicked prosper and traitors live at ease?
How long shall the wicked exult?

JEREMIAH 12:1B; PSALM 94:3B (NEB)

Children abused, atrocities condoned,
earthquakes, famines, terrorist attacks . . .

How long, O Lord, how long?

So much affliction horrifies us.
It is an outrage against our natural sense of justice,
and there are no pat answers or easy explanations.

Yet brokenness is at the heart of our Christian faith.

Jesus does not solve the mystery of suffering –
he enters it.

In Jesus, the darkness of the cross
meets the darkness of the world.

He bears our pain with us.

He has descended into hell out of love for us,
facing all the evil we can devise against him
and enduring the agony of total abandonment and desolation.

He is still crucified
wherever people are broken or in despair.
And he challenges us
to be more aware of the sufferings of others,
and to work for a fairer, gentler world.

Do you wish to honour the Body of Christ? Then do not disdain him when you see him in rags. After having honoured him in church with silken vestments do not leave him to die of cold outside for lack of clothing. For it is the same Jesus who says, 'This is my body,' and who says, 'You saw me hungry and did not give me to eat. What you have refused to the least of these my little ones, you have refused it to me.' The Body of Christ in the Eucharist demands pure souls, not costly garments. But in the poor he demands all our care.

ST JOHN CHRYSOSTOM (C.347–407)

A WORD FOR WEAVING:
How long, O Lord?

27. THE WILL OF GOD

'Not my will but yours be done.'
WORDS OF JESUS IN LUKE 22:42B

It is sometimes assumed that the will of God must, by definition, be the most unpleasant prospect imaginable.

Not so!

It is clear from the life and ministry of Jesus that God does not deliberately inflict suffering on people, as if misery were somehow good for us. On the contrary, Jesus was constantly working to relieve those he met from all kinds of burdens, diseases and troubles.

> God's will for us is God's desire for us.
> And God's delight is in enabling us to blossom
> and become the persons we were made to be.
> This is where our deepest happiness lies.

Yet there is a paradox here. In order to discover our true potential, we may have to face costly and demanding challenges. And we may need to be released from the power of selfishness and the false securities that can dominate our lives.

'Those who want to save their life will lose it, and those who lose their life for my sake, and for the sake of the gospel, will save it.'
WORDS OF JESUS IN MARK 8:35

When we pray, 'Your will be done,' we are asking God to dissolve everything that prevents us from serving him whole-heartedly. We are placing our will in the desire of a loving Creator, who is always drawing us into his work in the world.

Passionate, Creator God,
I place my will in yours.
Show me your delight in me
and your desire for me.
Guide my life towards you,
and teach me how to give myself,
and thus to find myself.

A WORD FOR WEAVING:
Your will be done.

28. 'CAN YOU DRINK THIS CUP?'

Jesus said to them ... 'Can you drink the cup that I must
drink, or be baptised with the baptism with which I must
be baptised?'

MARK 10:38–39 (JB)

Christian discipleship can be tough.

We are sometimes asked to love, and go on loving, in extreme-
ly difficult circumstances, with the love that 'bears all things,
believes all things, hopes all things, endures all things' (1
Corinthians 13:7).

Jesus tells us to forgive seventy times seven times, into infinity
(cf. Matthew 18:22, RSV). That is how God loves us – and he
asks no less of us in return.

This is costly. It would be much easier if forgiveness automati-
cally removed all the messy and uncomfortable things in life, or
if God would balance the scales so that everything became
absolutely fair.

But it is never like that.

* * *

Jesus embarked on a way of loving that cost him everything.
Are we able to join him and follow his teaching in every cir-
cumstance of our lives? Can we drink his cup?

Not in our own strength.

But if we ask Christ into our hearts, and receive bread and wine in a spirit of trust and generosity, the Holy Spirit will work in us so that we glimpse the miracle of grace, in spite of ourselves.

It is when we die to ourselves that we find life in all its fullness.

We can only be ourselves as we are poured out in love for God and for others; such is our salvation.

JOHN HADLEY

To set the earth ablaze, O God,
your Son submitted to a baptism unto death,
and from his cup of suffering
you call the Church to drink.
Keep our eyes fixed on Jesus
and give us strength in time of trial
to run the race that lies before us.
OPENING PRAYERS – THE ICEL COLLECTS

A WORD FOR WEAVING:
Lord, give us strength to drink your cup.

PART 3

'TAKE THIS CUP OF MY LIFE'

The Cup of Openness

O Lord,
take this cup,
this empty vessel of my life,
as my gift
brought to your table
without conditions.

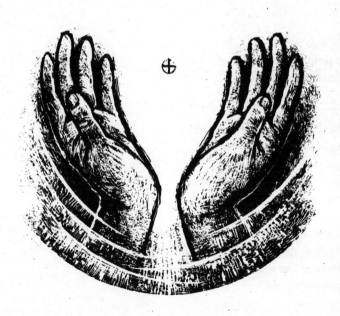

29. EARTHEN VESSELS

It is the same God that said, 'Let there be light shining out of darkness', who has shone in our minds to radiate the light of the knowledge of God's glory, the glory on the face of Christ.
We are only the earthenware jars that hold this treasure, to make it clear that such an overwhelming power comes from God and not from us.

2 Corinthians 4:6–7 (JB)

Father, take this cup of my life,
with all its blemishes,
stains
and cracks.

You do not ask me to be
a perfectly polished vessel,
flawless and dazzling.

But you do ask for my consent
to let you mend and restore me.

So I place myself in your hands
in complete trust.
I give you my contradictions and weaknesses,
and my failures to be like you,
knowing that you will cherish the gift
and cleanse me,

making my life reflect a little more
the brightness of your gospel
and the glory on the face of Christ.

Lord, fill me with the sparkling wine of your presence.

A WORD FOR WEAVING:
Take this cup of my life, Lord.

30. THE POTTER

The word that came to Jeremiah from the Lord: 'Come, go down to the potter's house, and there I will let you hear my words.'

JEREMIAH 18:1

Prompted by God, Jeremiah goes to watch the potter at work.

If the pot is not taking shape as intended, the potter starts again and remakes it.

'Can I not do with you, O house of Israel, just as this potter has done?' says the Lord. 'Just like the clay in the potter's hand, so are you in my hand, O house of Israel.'

JEREMIAH 18:6

We may find the process of being re-formed by God bewildering and painful. We have to trust that God knows what he is doing, and surrender ourselves totally into his hands.

Love waits to strengthen
Love waits to nourish
Love waits to be received
Love waits to heal

in time
the cup will be mended
in time
the cup will be raised
in time
the cup will receive again

in time
in time

JOYCE RUPP

A WORD FOR WEAVING:
Lord, you are the Potter, I am the clay.

31. GOD NEEDS EMPTY VESSELS

'Two men went up to the temple to pray, one a Pharisee and the other a tax collector. The Pharisee, standing by himself, prayed, "O God, I thank you that I am not like other people, I fast twice a week, I tithe . . ."
But the tax collector, standing far off, would not even look up to heaven, but beat his breast saying, "God, be merciful to me, a sinner!" I tell you, it was this man who went home right with God, rather than the other.'

BASED ON LUKE 18:11–14A

God needs empty vessels, not ones that are cluttered up with achievements and self-righteousness.

It is when we are 'poor in spirit' and know how much we need God that we are able to receive his grace.

Mercifully, the areas in our lives which we feel to be most unworthy can become the places where God works most powerfully in us.

Whenever we genuinely ask God for help, grace is there in the asking.

Come to this sacred table,
not because you must but because you may;

come, not to declare that you are righteous,
but that you desire to be true disciples of our Lord
  Jesus Christ;
come, not because you are strong,
but because you are weak;

not because you have any claim on heaven's rewards,
but because, in your frailty and sin,
you stand in constant need of heaven's mercy and help.

HOLY COMMUNION FOR LENT AND PASSIONTIDE,
THE METHODIST WORSHIP BOOK

Behold, Lord, an empty vessel that needs to be filled . . .
I am weak in the faith; strengthen me.
I am cold in love; warm me
that my love may go out to my neighbour.
I do not have a strong and firm faith;
at times I doubt and am unable to trust you altogether.
O Lord, help me. Strengthen my faith and trust in you.

MARTIN LUTHER (1483–1546)

A WORD FOR WEAVING:
Lord empty me of pride; fill me with yourself.

32. UNPROTECTED LOVE

The word of God is living and active, sharper than any two-edged sword, piercing until it divides soul from spirit, joints from marrow; it is able to judge the thoughts and intentions of the heart.

HEBREWS 4:12

To open ourselves to God in prayer
is to risk being vulnerable.

Prayer is unprotected love.

God knows,
with the finest sensitivity,
how each of us needs to be challenged and changed.

Yet prayer is a safe and secure place
in which to expose to God everything that we are,
because we are so deeply loved by him.

Corporate worship is also a kind of unprotected love,
as we gather to meet the One
who knows our inmost hearts
and desires to take possession of us.

In the foolishness of the divine love
Jesus was laid bare for us on the cross.
Are we prepared, for our part,
to lay open to him our deepest being,
in the radical offering of ourselves
that underlies all prayer and worship?

A WORD FOR WEAVING:
Before you, Lord.

33. THE WOUND OF LOVE

Upon my bed at night I sought him whom my soul loves;
I sought him, but found him not; I called him, but he
gave no answer.

Song of Solomon 3:1

All I can do, O God,
is open to you
the yearning, aching void in my heart
and ask you to fill it with yourself.

O divine Lover,
my soul thirsts and longs for you.

Because I am made in your likeness
you placed in me the desire for intimacy
that is also in you.
The wound of my longing
is also the wound of your longing for me, O God.

Draw me closer to you;
penetrate my restlessness
with your calm presence,
and show me, moment by moment,
how I must act,
when I must speak,
and when silence is better.

God says:
I know you are a frail vessel,
but I want to communicate with you
and be united to your sorrows.
Supporting you, I will save you.

HILDEGARD OF BINGEN (1098–1179)

A WORD FOR WEAVING:
O divine Lover, fill me with yourself.

34. LEARNING TO RECEIVE

I pray that you may know the love of Christ that sur-
passes knowledge, so that you may be filled with all the
fullness of God.

EPHESIANS 3:18A,19

We tend to think of church-going as a religious activity that *we do* for an hour on Sundays. But there is much more to it than that.

Worship is primarily something that *God is doing* in and among us.

It is true that we have gathered in order to honour God, and that worship is an offering of love for him.

But the initiative is God's. He has begun the conversation, in Scripture, in history, in creation and, supremely, in Jesus. We are simply responding.

God is the host at the Eucharist. We are not inviting God. It is God who invites us!

So we need to learn how to receive, to be passive as well as active in our worship, yielding ourselves to the divine action and allowing space for God to be God in us.

The Holy Spirit was already at work even before we began to think about coming to church, nudging, encouraging and drawing us there. During the worship itself, the Spirit contin-ues to work, sometimes in ways of which we are hardly aware, and sometimes sweeping us off our feet.

O Holy Spirit of God,
come into my heart and fill me:
I open the window of my soul to let you in.
Come and possess me, fill me with light and truth.
Of myself I am an empty vessel.
I offer to you the one thing I really possess,
my capacity for being filled by you.

ANON.

A WORD FOR WEAVING:
Make me receptive to you, O Lord.

35. WATER AND WINE

One of the soldiers pierced his side with a spear, and at once blood and water came out.

JOHN 19:34

This mindless act, violating the body of Jesus, has become for us a sign of hope and healing. The water and blood pouring out of Christ's side symbolize new life coming out of death, and remind us of the gifts of Baptism and Eucharist.

For this reason a little water is added to the wine at the Eucharist in some churches.

There is more. Wine represents divinity, and water humanity. When Jesus changed water into wine at the wedding of Cana, the Gospel writer, St John, saw this as a 'sign' that Jesus transforms the water of our humanity into the wine of his divine presence and glory (John 2:11).

By making the mixture in the chalice, we celebrate the mingling of human and divine in Jesus, and the mingling of his life with ours now:

Abide in me as I abide in you. As the Father has loved me, so I have loved you; abide in my love.

WORDS OF JESUS IN JOHN 15:4A, 9

Since we were made in the divine image, we should not be surprised that something of God can be found in us. By the sheer gift of grace, we can become what St Peter calls 'participants of the divine nature' (2 Peter 1:4), and find ourselves taken up into the dynamic life and love of the Trinity itself.

When we pray, the Spirit guides and enters our prayers, and we are united with Jesus as we reach out in love to the Father.

Our part is simply to be open to this incredible gift of the divine life flowing in and through us.

Jesus, permeate my heart and mind,
my attitudes and desires,
my behaviour and actions.

Help me to see the world
and other people
as you do.

Come into the centre of my being;
fill me with your Spirit
and pray in me to the Father.
Live in me, and I in you.

A WORD FOR WEAVING:
'Abide in me, and I in you.'

36. THE CUP OF THANKSGIVING

What shall I return to the Lord for all his bounty to me?
I will offer to you a thanksgiving sacrifice
and call on the name of the Lord.

PSALM 116:12,17

St Paul recommends that we should 'give thanks in all circum-stances' (1 Thessalonians 5:18a). But this is not always easy, and could seem a strange or naive way to behave.

Certainly the last thing we want when we have a bad headache is to be informed by pious friends that we should thank God for it.

Nevertheless, there is much wisdom in the practice of giving thanks for what is good in any particular situation. Doing this can release a positive, healing energy into our awareness, and transform the way in which we respond to whatever life brings.

Modern Western society badly needs a gentle spirit of grati-tude, to counteract our often strident concern with rights, claims and compensations.

'Eucharist' means 'thanksgiving'. A fundamental disposition of thankfulness may help us to be less restless and distracted, and more aware of God's good presence in all things, even in the harsh places.

It is immensely liberating to give thanks.
FRANCES YOUNG

What can we give to the Lord for all his goodness to us?
We offer our cup of praise,
brimful and bubbling over,
sparkling with honour, glory, praise,
wonder, tears and laughter,
in the love of the God
who created us to love him,
who gave his Son to restore us to our true selves,
and leads us now
as a thanks-giving people,
through life and death
into the dance of eternity . . .

A WORD FOR WEAVING:
'Give thanks in all circumstances.'

37. BODILY WORSHIP

And the Word became flesh and lived among us.

JOHN 1:14

Jesus was flesh and blood as we are, the only fully human person ever to have lived. St John, writing in his first Epistle, is anxious to stress that the life of Jesus was a totally physical reality:

> *We declare to you what was from the beginning, what we have heard, what we have seen with our eyes, what we have looked at and touched with our hands, concerning the word of life . . .*

1 JOHN 1:1

In the Eucharist we respond to Jesus' becoming flesh, or 'incarnation', as bodily people ourselves:

> speaking and singing,
> seeing and moving,
> tasting and touching,
> eating and drinking,
> smelling flowers or incense,
> and making physical gestures – such as standing,
> kneeling, shaking hands,
> or making the sign of the cross.

Worship is far more than words. In this encounter with our risen Lord we engage with the whole of ourselves, body, mind and spirit:

> *Jesus, beloved Lord,*
> *as we come together to wait upon you*
> *and to unite our voices in prayer and praise,*
> *bless the actions and words that we offer.*

Jesus, beloved Lord,
as I cup my hands to receive the bread,
take this empty vessel of my life
and fill me with yourself.

As a result of our meeting with God in the ordinary things of the Eucharist, every part of our existence, including its physical and material aspects, can be touched and changed:

Strengthen for service, Lord, the hands that have taken holy things;
may the ears which have heard your word be deaf to clamour
and dispute;
may the tongues which have sung your praise be free from deceit;
may the eyes which have seen the tokens of your love
shine with the light of hope;
and may the bodies which have been fed with your body
be refreshed with the fullness of your life.

MALABAR LITURGY

A WORD FOR WEAVING:
With my body I worship you, Lord.

38. CO-CREATORS WITH GOD

Praise the Lord! Praise him with trumpet sound; praise him with lute and harp!
Praise him with tambourine and dance; praise him with strings and pipe!

PSALM 150:1A, 3–4

In Christian worship we gather to share and offer our God-given creativity, to the glory of God and for the enrichment of each other.

As humans we best express our desire for God and our praise and thanksgiving, in music and poetry, beautiful buildings, stone, glass and wood, candles and colour, pictures and icons, dance and banners, embroidery, tapestry and flowers.

These creative gifts are better vehicles for our communion and conversation with God than discursive prose or logical analysis.

Composers, liturgists, architects and numerous other artists have poured a great deal of themselves into the gifts which have been handed on to us. When we worship we enter into their creativity, and they touch our lives in ways they would probably never have imagined.

The creative arts draw us into an attentiveness to the present moment, helping us to engage with worship at a deep level of ourselves.

* * *

Although there is a strong dramatic element to the Eucharist,

97

our worship is never a performance or concert given to a passive audience.

We are all involved. We all participate, not only by 'doing things' like reading lessons, but also by joining in, listening, seeing, and praying the words that are said or sung.

Our offering will always be flawed, because it is human, and church is a safe place in which to make mistakes. Yet, at the same time, we need to offer our best to God, with sensitivity and careful attention to detail.

There is hidden treasure here. Through this corporate, creative activity of worship we ourselves are mysteriously re-created and re-made, in the wonderful mingling of God's creativity with ours.

Encounters with God, no matter the time or place, cause eruptions of poetry, art, music and dance. Theology floats, flies, sings, dances, declaims, and decorates the world, as well as arguing for clarity, conviction and conversion.

JOSEPH A BROWN SJ

WORD FOR WEAVING:
O worship the Lord in the beauty of holiness!

39. FOOLS FOR CHRIST

If you think that you are wise in this age, you should become fools so that you may become wise. For the wisdom of this world is foolishness with God.

1 Corinthians 3:18b–19a

Christian worship can seem strange, even extravagant.

When we use beautiful buildings and fine music for worship, we are like the woman who poured expensive perfume over the head of Jesus, risking criticism and incomprehension from those who would say, 'What a waste! Why not give the money to the poor?'

Worship, like the creative arts, is for its own sake.
It does not exist for a purpose outside itself, such as productivity or usefulness.
Nor can its value be measured in a test-tube or assessed on a balance-sheet.

Yet its worth is unsurpassed, and its fruits are infinite.

So we follow the foolishness of God rather than the wisdom of the world, and continue to devote energy and attention to our worship, gloriously 'wasting' time (as some would see it) in this encounter with our extravagantly generous God.

In 1918 the great liturgical scholar, Romano Guardini, likened Christian liturgical worship to the play of the child and the creation of the artist:

To be at play, or to fashion a work of art in God's sight ... such is the essence of liturgy. From this is derived its sublime mingling of profound earnestness and divine joyfulness.

And in the Book of Proverbs, Chapter 8, Wisdom is personified and says:

'Yahweh created me when his purpose first unfolded,
    before the oldest of his works.
I was by his side, a master craftsman,
    delighting him day after day,
ever at play in his presence,
    at play everywhere in his world . . .'

PROVERBS 8:22, 30–31A (JB)

This passage conveys a sense of a playfulness and delight at the heart of God's creation. It is good to echo this in our attitude to worship, and not to be afraid either to enjoy our liturgy or to pour our best resources into it.

The Christian life . . . should be marked by an incurable seriousness and an incurable lightness.

JOHN DRURY

A WORD FOR WEAVING:
We are fools for Christ's sake.

40. LETTING GO

For you have died, and your life is hidden with Christ in God.

COLOSSIANS 3:3

At Holy Communion, the person who celebrates on behalf of us all, needs, in a sense, to disappear into the Eucharist.

Those of us who are gathered round the table are also called to let ourselves go into the presence of the risen Christ, so that we may be formed and changed by him.

It is through this self-abandonment that we can find our true worth, not through our own merit, but because of our God-given capacity to receive the divine life within us.

This is the mystery of prayer and sacrament.

The bread and wine of the Eucharist will disappear into us. At the same time we are invited to lose ourselves in Christ, and, in so doing, find ourselves.

Take, Lord, as your right, and receive as my gift,
all my freedom, my memory,
my understanding and my will.
Whatever I am and whatever I possess,
you have given to me;
I restore it all to you again,
to be at your disposal,
according to your will.
Give me only a love for you,

and the gift of your grace;
then I am rich enough,
and ask for nothing more.
    ST IGNATIUS LOYOLA (1491–1556)

A WORD FOR WEAVING:
Let me lose myself in you, Lord.

41. LISTEN!

Be still, and know that I am God!

PSALM 46:10A

God help me the moment
My heart starts opening
To comprehend and give.
I will be born in that hour of grace.
I will begin to live.

BRENDAN KENNELLY

The Eucharist shows us how much God desires to open the world up to himself.

But how open and available are we to God?

We need an emptiness in our soul.

We need a clear space inside us where God can surprise and challenge us, and free us from our preconceived ideas and habitual streams of thoughts.

Relax the tension in your neck, shoulders, and the rest of your body.
Become aware of your breathing, and listen to the sounds around you.
Ask God to fill you with his peace.
Rest in his presence, and absorb his light and love with each breath that you take.
If it helps you to focus, repeat the name of Jesus to yourself quietly and slowly, especially when your mind has wandered off.
Be still and know.

The very familiarity of the liturgy, and the mental chatter buzzing through our brains, can make it difficult to concentrate during worship. The more we pray quietly in the rest of our lives, the more chance we have of being able to recollect ourselves and be inwardly attentive when we are in church.

The still centre at the depth of our being is holy ground. It is the 'inner room' where we are alone with God, in singleness of mind and heart, with no agenda other than to be receptive to him (Matthew 6:6).

Communal, prayerful silence in church worship is a rich experience that is often neglected, not least at the start of a service. This is not to deny the value of friendly conversations when people first come into church. But perhaps we need to be bold, and invite worshippers to spend a moment in quietness together immediately before worship begins (ideally after the notices, if those come at the beginning of the service). The noise of small children is not necessarily a disturbance, but can be part of this shared moment of reverent anticipation, as we prepare to meet our God.

In the silence and stillness
let us open our hearts and lives to God,
that we may be prepared for his coming
as Light and Word, as Bread and Wine.
HOLY COMMUNION FOR CHRISTMAS AND EPIPHANY,
THE METHODIST WORSHIP BOOK

A WORD FOR WEAVING:
Be still and know

PART 4

THE SHAPE OF EUCHARISTIC WORSHIP

The shape of the Eucharist forms a coherent sequence, and is like a journey of faith that we undertake together. The two high points are the reading of the Gospel and the distribution of bread and wine. Each of these reflects the two great things that God offers to us in Jesus: he shares our life, and he transforms it.

First we gather together, bringing our own stories with us, and we are formed into a community of worshippers. In Scripture we engage with God's conversation with us, and, in the Gospel, we encounter Jesus who has entered our life.

Then we offer our grateful response to what Jesus has done. We open ourselves up to his transforming power and receive bread and wine, a sign and pledge of Jesus' ongoing life in us.

Finally we are sent out into the world to be bearers of the divine love in all that we do and are.

Gathering for Worship (42)
Prayers of Penitence and Reconciliation (43)
The Gloria (44)
The Collect and Moments of Quiet (45)
Scripture and Sermon (46)
The Creed or 'Affirmation of Faith' (47)
Intercession (48)
The Exchange of the Peace (49)
The Preparation of the Table I, II (50–51)

The Eucharistic Prayer:

I: The Opening Dialogue (52)
II: The Story of our Salvation (53)
III: 'Holy, holy, holy!' (54)

42. FORMED INTO COMMUNITY

Gathering for Worship

For just as the body is one and has many members, and all the members of the body, though many, are one body, so it is with Christ. For in the one Spirit we were all baptized into one body.

1 CORINTHIANS 12:12–13A

We belong to each other when we worship together.

We are not like a cluster of separate tubes, each connecting a person to God but without any interaction between them. A new entity is born when we come to church, similar to the way in which individual singing-voices become a choir.

So we begin the Eucharist by greeting each other in the name of the Lord, as a way of affirming our mutual commitment:

The Lord be with you   or: Grace, mercy and peace
and also with you.   from God our Father
                           and the Lord Jesus Christ
                           be with you
                           and also with you.

This greeting is not just a minor preliminary, but sets the scene as we move into the opening parts of the liturgy that will form us into a community:

- an act of penitence and absolution
- singing 'Glory to God!' with the angels
- gathering our prayers together in the opening Collect.

Throughout the service, the Holy Spirit takes the prayerfulness of each of us, and moulds us into a praying and worshipping assembly, the Body of Christ.

During church services we support each other, especially if someone is going through a bad time, and needs to be held and carried by the worship of the group. We affect and depend on each other more than we realise, and we never know when God might use our own praying, inadequate though it may feel, to help somebody else.

Our knowledge of God as Trinity – the Father, the Son and the Holy Spirit in loving communion with each other – reminds us that we too are called into a loving relationship with one another.

A WORD FOR WEAVING:
Pray for unity of the Spirit in the bond of peace.

43. OUR FORGIVING GOD

Prayers of Penitence and Reconciliation

The Lord is merciful and gracious, slow to anger and abounding in steadfast love.

PSALM 103:8

Most merciful God . . .
We have not loved you with our whole heart.
We have not loved our neighbours as ourselves.
In your mercy
forgive what we have been,
help us to amend what we are,
and direct what we shall be;
that we may do justly, love mercy,
and walk humbly with you, our God. Amen.

HOLY COMMUNION, ORDER ONE, *COMMON WORSHIP*

Jesus challenges two of the greatest enemies to human wholeness: despair and complacency.

Despair can paralyse us
with a terrible fear of not being good enough for God.
But there is no need.

None of us is ever worthy to approach God.
Yet God graciously invites us
to his feast of word and sacrament,
treating us as kindly
as a parent encouraging a small child to walk (Hosea 11:1–4).

God never loses hope in us
but waits to welcome and embrace us,
inviting us to come as we are,
not as we think we ought to be.

Our God is a forgiving – literally 'for-giving' – God.
When we abandon our complacency
and acknowledge our self-deceptions and failings,
God gently wipes our faces clean
and pours his mercy into our mistakes.

Bread and wine confirm the gift of the divine mercy,
as we respond to his tender command,
  'Take and eat. Take and drink.
  This is for the forgiveness of your sins.'

God of gentleness and strength,
source of our being and wellspring of compassion,
we offer you our sorrow for our sins
and our desire to forgive each other.
Open our hearts to your inflowing mercy.

If anyone is in Christ, there is a new creation: everything
old has passed away; see, everything has become new!
                                            2 CORINTHIANS 5:17

A WORD FOR WEAVING:
Kyrie eleison! **Lord, make us whole!**

44. GLORY TO GOD!

The Gloria

Then an angel of the Lord stood before them, and the glory of the Lord shone around them, and they were terrified. And suddenly there was with the angel a multitude of the heavenly host, praising God and saying, 'Glory to God in the highest heaven, and on earth peace, good will among people!'

LUKE 2:9, 13–14

We now tap into the ceaseless praise and worship of the angelic hosts in heaven, echoing the words that stunned the shepherds in the Christmas story:

Glory to God in the highest,
and peace to his people on earth.

In our mind's eye we can allow ourselves to bathe in the translucent light that flooded the fields outside Bethlehem, similar to the radiance that Peter, James and John saw when Jesus was transfigured before them (Mark 9:2–8).

This is a moment of mystery, a glimpse of transcendence, a song of delight.

We praise you for your glory!

Angels, I read, belong to nine different orders. Seraphs are the highest; they are aflame with love for God, and stand closer to him than the others. Seraphs love God . . . The seraphs are born of a stream of fire issuing from under God's throne. They are, according to Dionysius the Areopagite, 'all wings', having, as Isaiah notes, six wings apiece, two of which they fold over their eyes. Moving perpetually toward God, they perpetually praise him, crying, 'Holy, Holy, Holy . . .' But according to some rabbinic writings, they can sing only the first 'Holy' before the intensity of their love ignites them and dissolves them again, perpetually, into flames.

ANNIE DILLARD

A WORD FOR WEAVING
Glory to God in the highest!

45. WORDS PLACED IN SILENCE

The Collect and Moments of Quiet

Take heed, be quiet, do not fear . . .
ISAIAH 7:4A

Almighty God,
you have made us for yourself,
and our hearts are restless till they find their rest in you:
pour your love into our hearts and draw us to yourself,
and so bring us at last to your heavenly city
where we shall see you face to face.
FROM THE COLLECT FOR THE SEVENTEENTH SUNDAY
AFTER TRINITY, COMMON WORSHIP

As music needs pauses,

and poetry needs white space around it,

our worship needs moments of quietness,
so that our words have room to breathe
within the flow of the liturgy.

A time of quiet before the prayer of penitence
helps us to gather our scattered thoughts
and remind ourselves that we are in the presence of God.

There may also be a pause before the Collect,
the prayer which draws together the aspirations
of everyone present.

Silence can also follow the Scripture readings,
giving us a chance to 'mark, learn and inwardly digest'
what we have heard.

In the end, all our words concerning God
lead us into a mystery that we can never fully grasp.

Silence surrounds the Eucharist itself,
and it is good to ponder this gift
in a moment of stillness together
at the end of the Eucharistic Prayer,
or after receiving Communion.

> Liturgical silence is purposeful, pregnant, and controlled – the thunderous quiet of people communicating that which escapes being put into words.
>
> AIDAN KAVANAGH

Let all mortal flesh keep silence
And with fear and trembling stand;
Ponder nothing earthly-minded,
For with blessing in his hand
Christ our God to earth descendeth,
Our full homage to demand.

LITURGY OF ST JAMES, TRANS. G. MOULTRIE.

A WORD FOR WEAVING:
My soul waits in silence.

46. THE BREAKING OF THE WORD

Scripture and Sermon

For as the rain and snow come down from heaven, and do not return there until they have watered the earth, so shall my word be that goes out from my mouth; it shall not return to me empty, but it shall accomplish that which I purpose.

ISAIAH 55:10A,11.

The gift of the Word comes before the gifts of bread and wine in the Eucharist.

Bible readings are not a relic from the past, fossilized and fixed in a single interpretation. In prayer and worship Scripture becomes the living word of God for us now, as the Holy Spirit makes connections between our story and the story of salvation.

Jesus himself will have prayed the Psalms and read the Scriptures which form our Old Testament. When a Psalm comes after an Old Testament reading, this is a prayerful response of heart and soul to what we have just heard.

The climax of the Bible readings is the Gospel, where we meet Jesus face to face, and, in some churches, greet him by standing and singing, 'Alleluia!'

In the Eastern Orthodox Liturgy of St John Chrysostom, the following words are said by the priest just before the reading of the Gospel:

O Master, you love all people;
make the spotless light of your divine wisdom
  shine in our hearts,
and open the eyes of our mind to an understanding
  of the things you teach us in your gospel.

And the deacon then sings aloud:

Let us attend!

Let us attend! Let us listen to the Word from a deep place within ourselves, and allow its impact to descend from our head to our heart.

> Solemn reading requires solemn listening, not simultaneous reading. Otherwise, why read aloud at all? Our bookish upbringing encourages people to read when they should listen. As a result, the poetry has lost its power, for its resonant, wise, fervent and festive language is meant to be heard.
> … [Let] the sacred word unfold in its full spiritual-corporeal reality and soar through space to the listener, to be heard and received into his life.
>
> ROMERO GUARDINI

In the homily or sermon (sometimes aided by drama, imaginative meditation or pictures), our souls are fed by reflection and teaching based on the words of Scripture. This breaking of the word foreshadows the breaking of bread that is still to come.

Word and sacrament throw light on each other.

A WORD FOR WEAVING:
Open my heart to your Word.

47. WE BELIEVE

The Creed or 'Affirmation of Faith'

'I believe; help my unbelief!'
                                    MARK 9:24.

How can you put into formulas and definitions the arrival of God among us in the man Jesus?

You can't!

And yet we have to try, not only to protect our faith from distortion and misunderstanding, but also to give us guidelines and springboards from which to jump into the unknown territory of life with God.

In the creeds we declare our willingness to stand up and be counted as believers.

We believe in one God . . .

This is not just a series of doctrines demanding intellectual assent. It is also a way of expressing our commitment to our Christ-like God. Like the early church fathers who laboured hard and long to produce our creeds, we find ourselves wrestling with words to describe the indescribable.

In the fourth century the theologian Hilary of Poitiers (c. 315–67) wrote:

The errors of heretics and blasphemers force us to scale perilous heights, to speak unutterable words, to trespass on forbidden ground.

Faith ought in silence to fulfil the commandments, worshipping the Father, reverencing with him the Son, abounding in the Holy Spirit; but we must strain the poor resources of our language to express thoughts too great for words.

The error of others compels us to err in daring to embody in human terms truths which ought to be hidden in the silent veneration of the heart.

The Creed celebrates the gifts of creation and salvation. Although the words often trip lightly off the tongue, and may feel tedious through much repetition, many of the phrases can lead into silent adoration. It is worth spending time meditating on key phrases:

maker of all that is, seen and unseen

God from God

Light from Light

true God from true God . . .

. . . this is Jesus of Nazareth, the Risen One, who is among us now and sends his Spirit into our hearts to draw us into loving communion with the Father!

The Nicene Creed, generally used on Sundays, is not the church's last word, but it is an important word. It was the best way the fourth century Christians could find to hold together the paradox of Jesus' being both human and divine. The first disciples had experienced this paradox as a powerful reality. But to set it down in logical sentences, against those who would distort the truth, proved a massive challenge.

Thus the Creed is a gift, albeit imperfect, passed on to us from our forebears in the faith.

We may struggle with its language and definitions. But it is a place where we can rededicate ourselves to the life-time's task of seeking the God who always eludes us yet is intimately close.

A WORD FOR WEAVING:
We believe!

48. PRAYING FOR OTHERS

Intercession

In the power of the Spirit and in union with Christ, let us pray to the Father.

FORMS OF INTERCESSION, *COMMON WORSHIP*

Interceding is not reminding God of his duties, it is taking a step towards the heart of the world . . . We must never in any way try to manipulate God's purposes for those for whom we pray but, giving ourselves unconditionally to God, be instruments to be used as he wills, making a space in which divine love can surround the person for whom we pray.

MOTHER MARY CLARE SLG

The Intercessions in church gather up the prayers of the whole assembly, not in long lists of information, but in clear, well-directed words that focus and represent the concerns of each person present.

We offer our intercession for our fellow human beings, holding them in the divine light and mercy, and praying that the love which God pours so generously into us may overflow to the farthest ends of the earth.

We also acknowledge before God our own responsibility for the pain of the world. Whether we like it or not, we are all involved in the systems and attitudes that cause so much misery and injustice.

We do not only pray for people who are in trouble. Our neighbours, friends and colleagues are woven into our prayers too, as we seek to align our small energy of desire with God's great energy of love for the world.

The whole act of worship is for the sake of the world as well as for ourselves, and it is not just in the 'intercession slot' that we are praying for others. We bring our communities with us in our hearts and minds whenever we come to church, and we represent all humanity before God, praying on their behalf in the priesthood of all believers (see 1 Peter 2:5).

Work your miracle of love in and through us, O God,
so that your compassion
may become a stream of blessing,
flowing out of our lives into our communities,
and into the places where healing, hope and peace
are most needed.

A WORD FOR WEAVING:
Loving Lord, use our prayer.

49. 'PEACE BE WITH YOU'

The Exchange of the Peace

Be united; live in peace, and the God of love and peace will be with you. Greet one another with the holy kiss.
ST PAUL IN 2 CORINTHIANS 13:11B, 12A (JB)

As the Lord has greeted us, so now we greet each other.

***The peace of the Lord be always with you
and also with you.***

If we are honest, we will never exchange the Peace in a state of perfect harmony and affection. Yet that does not mean that we are being hypocritical.

It is the Peace of *Christ* that we are calling down on each other, not just something of our own.

The Peace, like the whole Eucharist, is a glimpse and pledge of the ultimate peace of God's kingdom. So we place our incompleteness within the completeness of God's love, and express our desire for unity with each other by exchanging this sign of friendship.

For those who face constant hostility and tension in daily life, the moment when fellow worshippers turn round, grasp their hand, look them in the eye and say, 'Peace be with you,' can be the one thing that gets them through the week.

* * *

The Eucharist is itself the supreme sign of our unity in Christ, transcending all denominational barriers. The angels will surely dance when members of the various Christian churches can fully and freely share this sacrament with each other.

Thus it is with the wine.
Remember, friends, how wine is made –
individual grapes hang together in a bunch,
but the juice from them all is mingled
    to become a single brew.
This is the image chosen by Christ our Lord
to show how, at his own table,
the mystery of our unity and peace
    is solemnly consecrated.

ST AUGUSTINE OF HIPPO (354–430)

Generous God,
we offer you our life together.
Help us mend our fractured communion,
and show us how to receive the unity
that you long to give us.

A WORD FOR WEAVING:
That we may be one.

50. OFFERING OUR ORDINARINESS

The Preparation of the Table I

> *I appeal to you therefore, brothers and sisters, by the mercies of God, to present your bodies as a living sacrifice, holy and acceptable to God, which is your spiritual worship.*

> ROMANS 12:1

Bread and wine are basic ingredients of daily life. When we bring these and our gifts of money to the Eucharistic table (in what is traditionally known as the Offertory) we are offering to God our life in all its ordinariness.

Going to church does not mean leaving behind the unspectacular parts of ourselves, as if we should only present to God the 'Sunday best' of our personal lives. Even the most mundane aspects of our experience will be touched and sanctified by this meeting with the risen Lord.

God has given us the gift of life and we now return our whole selves to him: our talents and skills, our work and leisure, our struggles and desires, our failures and successes. We also offer the world of which we are a part.

All things come from you, O Lord, and of your own do we give you.

Everything can be offered.
Everything can be redeemed and used for good.

God receives our prayers of intercession
and gives them back to us
as blessings for the world.

God receives our gifts of bread and wine
and gives them back to us,
charged with new meaning.

God receives the offering of our lives
and gives them back to us,
renewed and transformed.

A WORD FOR WEAVING:
Here I am, Lord.

51. CELEBRATING CREATION

The Preparation of the Table II

Yours, Lord, is the greatness, the power,
the glory, the splendour, and the majesty;
for everything in heaven and on earth is yours.
All things come from you,
and of your own do we give you.
PRAYERS AT THE PREPARATION OF THE
COMMUNION TABLE, *COMMON WORSHIP*

It is as if
all creation is focused
in these simple elements
of bread and wine:
tokens of physical matter,
fruitfulness of earth,
abundance of beauty,
our fertile yet fragile world . . .

Blessed are you, O Lord our God,
Source of all creation,
still calling forth all that you have made,
and, behold, it is very good!

We thank you for bread and wine – grain and grape,
products of sun, rain and soil,
co-operation of our human labour
with your continual bounty.

Help us to reverence the gift of matter,
to grieve over our wanton greed and pollution,
and never to lose our sense of wonder
at the immensity of the universe
and the intricacy of this planet.

127

There are many imaginative ways of praising God for the gift of creation in our worship.

In some Indian churches, eight flowers are placed around the plate and cup on the altar, at the eight points of the compass, to show that the bread and wine represent the whole world.

In a church in the USA, after receiving the sacrament or a blessing, each person moves to a prayer area at the side which is full of pictures, newspaper cuttings, stones, shells and flowers; here they light a candle and offer a prayer of thanksgiving, sorrow or intercession.

REREDOS

The 'reredos' is the screen behind the altar, usually of stone or wood. But in this poem (set in the chapel of Bryn Mel on Anglesey) there is clear glass behind the altar, and the priest celebrating Communion has his back to the congregation.

The reredos was not
an ecclesiastical adornment
of symbols,
but plain glass,
with the danger
of distracting the celebrant
from
the properties of the communion table,

for
in the translucence
the green earth
budded in the morning view,
the river was in bloom,

128

the air a joyous flight,
and the sunshine
set the clouds ablaze,

and I noticed
the priest's eyes
as it were unconsciously
placing his hand
on these gifts,
as though these
were
the bread and the wine.

EUROS BOWEN

A WORD FOR WEAVING:
Blessed are you, O Lord our God, King of all creation!

THE EUCHARISTIC PRAYER

(also known as The Great Thanksgiving)

52. WITH DELIGHT WE JOIN IN THIS PRAYER

The Eucharistic Prayer I: The Opening Dialogue

The Lord be with you
and also with you.

Lift up your hearts.
We lift them to the Lord.

Let us give thanks to the Lord our God.
It is right to give thanks and praise.

HOLY COMMUNION, ORDER ONE, COMMON WORSHIP

This exchange between the minister and the congregation marks a crucial point in the liturgy, launching the Eucharistic prayer, or Great Thanksgiving, which is the climax of the whole service.

The dialogue reflects the fact that the whole assembly is celebrating, not just the person who is presiding.

The Lord be with you. **And also with you.**

We commit ourselves to pray for each other,
and affirm our unity
as the gathered people of Christ.

Lift up your hearts. **We lift them to the Lord.**

We allow our hearts to soar,
and lift everything that we are,
and all creation,
into the mystery of God.

Let us give thanks to the Lord our God. **It is right to give thanks and praise.**

Echoing the ancient responses of God's people,
we bless and thank our gracious Lord.

Thus, together, we reclaim the gift of our delight in God, and God's delight in us.

We stop trying to prove anything to God, and simply allow God's beauty and generosity to hold our attention and win our loving response.

A WORD FOR WEAVING:
We lift our hearts to the Lord!

53. A SACRIFICE OF THANKSGIVING

The Eucharistic Prayer II: The Story of our Salvation.

O give thanks to the LORD, call on his name,
*   make known his deeds among the peoples!*
Sing to him, sing praises to him;
*   tell of all his wonderful works.*

PSALM 105:1–2

The word 'Eucharist' is derived from the Greek word for 'thanksgiving', and each Eucharistic Prayer begins with an out-pouring of praise to God for his boundless goodness towards us.

We offer our sacrifice of thanksgiving in a sweeping narrative that recalls our creation and God's ongoing love for us, culminating in our final redemption in Jesus. Extra words of praise may be added to mark a particular season or special day.

Such a majestic stream of praise, which includes the *Sanctus* ('Holy, holy, holy'), forms a strong contrast to the simplicity of the Last Supper narrative that will follow.

You are worthy of our thanks and praise,
Lord God of truth,
for by the breath of your mouth
you have spoken your word,
and all things have come into being.

You fashioned us in your image
and placed us in the garden of your delight.
Though we chose the path of rebellion
you would not abandon your own.

. . . Embracing our humanity,
Jesus showed us the way of salvation;
loving us to the end,
he gave himself to death for us;
dying for his own,
he set us free from the bonds of sin,
that we might rise and reign with him in glory.

HOLY COMMUNION, EUCHARISTIC PRAYER F,
COMMON WORSHIP

A WORD FOR WEAVING:
We give you thanks and praise.

54. THE SONGS OF THE ANGELS

The Eucharistic Prayer III: 'Holy, holy, holy!'

Day and night without ceasing they sing, 'Holy, holy, holy, the Lord God the Almighty, who was and is and is to come.'

REVELATION 4:8B

As the Orthodox churches teach us, heaven comes down to meet the earth when we worship, and our prayers are taken up into the unceasing stream of praise of the angels and saints.

There are two glorious moments in the Eucharistic liturgy when we are especially caught up in the love of God, joining our song with the songs of the angels:

- *Glory to God in the highest!* has already echoed the angelic chorus in the fields of Bethlehem.

- Now our solemn exclamation, *Holy, holy, holy!* connects us with the worship of the communion of saints in heaven (Revelation 4:8–11).

Therefore with angels and archangels,
and with all the company of heaven,
we proclaim your great and glorious name . . .
EUCHARISTIC PRAYERS A, B AND C, *COMMON WORSHIP*

If the worshipping life of our local congregation sometimes feels small or insignificant, we can take heart from the fact that our services are part of the vast, living tapestry of worship that reaches across cultures and continents, beyond time and into eternity.

And so, with all the faithful of every time and place,
we join with choirs of angels in the eternal hymn:
Holy, holy, holy Lord . . .

HOLY COMMUNION FOR PENTECOST AND TIMES OF
RENEWAL, *THE METHODIST WORSHIP BOOK*

A WORD FOR WEAVING:
Lord, this is the gateway to heaven.

55. THE IMPORTANCE OF THE MEAL

The Eucharistic Prayer IV: Narrative of the Last Supper

On the night before he died, he came to supper with his friends.

EUCHARISTIC PRAYER G, *COMMON WORSHIP*

At a meal shared with others, we come together not only to nourish our bodies but also to participate in the face to face exchanges and conviviality which flow naturally around a table. The host has made careful preparations, and we give our attention to each other as well as to the food in front of us.

In New Testament times, to insult or betray somebody with whom you had broken bread was seen as a violation of human trust. That is why Jesus' sorrow was so intense when Judas had dipped his bread into the same dish as he had (Mark 14:18–21).

Early Christian communities used to celebrate the Eucharist in the context of a communal meal (see 1 Corinthians 11:17–34). Although we have generally lost this custom now, we can still benefit in our Eucharist from a sense of the sacredness of a meal taken together.

The imagery of the meal reminds us that the Eucharist is not a purely private or subjective affair. Each person is fed individually but also belongs to the wider group, in what is an essentially corporate activity.

Lord Jesus, courteous host,
help us to respect each other
as 'com-panions' – literally, 'bread-sharers',
and as fellow members of your Body.

A WORD FOR WEAVING:
We come gladly to your table.

56. 'WE REMEMBER'

The Eucharistic Prayer V: Remembering.

'Do this in remembrance of me.'

1 CORINTHIANS 11:25B

In the Bible, the act of remembering involves more than simply recalling events from the past. It is part of an ongoing relationship with God.

At the annual Passover Festival the Israelites remembered God's mighty act of bringing them out of Egypt and forming them into his own people. They reclaimed that gift of freedom for each subsequent generation, asking God to continue to remember and care for them.

Memory has the power to bring the past into our present experience. I once spoke with a consultant who encourages patients who are recovering from major surgery to recall and re-live good and beautiful things in their past lives, because doing this can enhance the healing process.

The Israelites themselves were sustained during their darkest moments in exile by reminding themselves of God's great love for them.

* * *

At Holy Communion we remember the story of God's mighty action in sending Jesus, and encounter this gift of love as a reality today.

When we take bread and wine, we are not just re-enacting or

commemorating an event that happened 2,000 years ago. We are opening ourselves to receive the presence and power of Jesus now.

And as we remember, we ourselves are *re-membered,* put together again and formed into the Body of Christ, people in whom Jesus is embodied in the world.

Our God is faithful and always remembers *us,* in his continuous movement of creating and gathering all things to himself.

'Jesus, remember me when you come into your kingdom.'
THE PENITENT THIEF, LUKE 23:42

A WORD FOR WEAVING:
With thankfulness we remember.

57. PENTECOST CONTINUES

The Eucharistic Prayer VI: Calling on the Holy Spirit

By this we know that we abide in him and he in us, because he has given us of his Spirit.

1 JOHN 4:13

In the Eucharistic prayer we call upon the Holy Spirit to sanctify *both* the gifts of bread *and* wine and ourselves as the community and Body of Christ.

It is not enough for the bread and wine to be transformed unless we ourselves are also willing to be changed and transformed into Christ's people on earth.

By the action of the Holy Spirit, the text of the Eucharist becomes a dialogue with the text of our lives now.

The gift of the Holy Spirit is not confined to the great event at Pentecost (Acts 2:1–13). The Spirit continues to gives us fresh insights, enabling us to make new connections between our daily experience and the person of Jesus.

The gathered community of worshippers, the living Word of Scripture, and the bread and wine, are all mysteriously charged with Christ's presence by the power of the Holy Spirit. If we are willing, all this can break us open to the purifying fire of his love, and to the startling value-system of a Master who serves his followers and asks everything in return.

Father, by your Holy Spirit
let these gifts of your creation be to us
the body and blood of our Lord Jesus Christ;
form us into the likeness of Christ
and make us a perfect offering in your sight.

EUCHARISTIC PRAYER F, *COMMON WORSHIP*

A WORD FOR WEAVING:
Come Holy Spirit!

58. OUR WHOLE-HEARTED 'YES!'

The Eucharistic Prayer VII: The Doxology and 'Great Amen'

> . . . *through Jesus Christ our Lord;*
> *by whom, and with whom, and in whom,*
> *in the unity of the Holy Spirit,*
> *all honour and glory be yours, almighty Father,*
> *for ever and ever.*
> *AMEN!*
>
> EUCHARISTIC PRAYERS B AND C, ORDER ONE,
> *COMMON WORSHIP*

The 'Great Amen'
is the most important Amen in the whole service.

It is the climax of the Eucharistic prayer,
coming after the tremendous swell of thankfulness
which forms the closing *doxology*
or 'expression of praise'.

In this Amen we acknowledge
the great things God has done for us,
and give our whole-hearted Yes
to welcome the One who comes among us.

Everyone present says or sings a hearty *'Amen!'*
because it is the entire assembly that celebrates the Eucharist.
We, the people, are giving our assent

to what the minister or priest
has said and done on our behalf.

The whole prayer consecrates,
and we all participate in it.

A WORD FOR WEAVING:
Amen! Alleluia!

59. 'ABBA, FATHER!'

The Lord's Prayer

Jesus said to them, 'When you pray, say: "Father, hallowed be your name. Your kingdom come." '

LUKE 11:2

Saying or singing the Lord's Prayer at this point is a good preparation for receiving Communion, although the prayer can appropriately come at other moments in the service too.

Jesus taught us to pray to our heavenly Father for our daily bread, for forgiveness, and for the grace to do God's will in the world. The whole prayer is an act of trust and surrender.

Some worshipping communities stretch out their arms when they say the Lord's Prayer, as a sign of their desire to be totally available to God.

Most of us would feel self-conscious doing that in church, but we can still do it when we pray alone.

Whenever we say, 'Our Father . . .,' we recall Jesus' own intimate prayer, 'Abba, Father' (see Mark 14:36) and ask for the grace to connect our own lives with God's continuing action of blessing the world.

A WORD FOR WEAVING:
Give us today our daily bread.

60. BROKEN BREAD, PEOPLE UNITED

Breaking the Bread

Because there is one bread, we who are many are one body, for we all partake of the one bread.

1 CORINTHIANS 10:17

The breaking of the bread
is a key moment in the Eucharist.

First we are reminded of how Jesus' body was broken for us,
and we acknowledge our part in the sinfulness that brought
him to crucifixion:

> *Lamb of God,*
> *you take away the sin of the world,*
> *have mercy on us.*

But it is not only Jesus' death that we proclaim,
because the broken bread leads us on
to celebrate the resurrection.

> For the two disciples
> who walked, unwittingly, with the risen Jesus
> on the road to Emmaus,
> the breaking of the bread before their eyes
> was the moment of recognition (Luke 24:13–35).
> The Master who had been crucified, was there,
> alive, among them!
> And Jesus affirms us now
> as friends and companions in his risen life.

Finally, the bread which is broken and distributed among us
is a symbol of our unity in the risen Lord.
We, who are fragmented, share the one loaf,
asking Christ to heal our divisions
and to draw us closer to each other
as his Body on earth.
This symbol is especially powerful
when we use a single loaf,
or large wafers that need to be broken for distribution.

As this broken bread was scattered over the mountains, and when brought together became one, so let your Church be brought together from the ends of the earth into your kingdom.

FROM A EUCHARISTIC LITURGY IN *THE DIDACHE*
(PROBABLY EARLY SECOND CENTURY)

Paradoxically,
it is Jesus' brokenness
that draws us together.

A WORD FOR WEAVING:
As one Body we share in the one bread.

61. THE GIFT

Receiving Holy Communion

'Unless you eat the flesh of the Son of Man and drink his blood, you have no life in you. For my flesh is true food and my blood is true drink.'

JOHN 6:53B, 55

Tenderly you call me,
freely you forgive me,
graciously you fill me.

Lord, make my life
into the place of your indwelling.

May I participate in your love,
and know your kingdom truly within me.

A WORD FOR WEAVING:
Fill me!

62. GO OUT!

The Sending Out I

Send us out in the power of your Spirit to live and work to your praise and glory.
HOLY COMMUNION, ORDER ONE, *COMMON WORSHIP*

An essential part of the Eucharist is the sending out of the assembly in the name of Christ.

Our worship has not been a cosy escape from reality, pulling us away from a proper engagement with the issues of world. On the contrary, we have brought everything that is most real to us into this encounter with God.

So now we are dismissed and sent to go about the Lord's business, to be filled with the same Spirit that filled him, and to witness to his love in our lives.

The root of the term 'Mass' is the Latin word *missum*, which means, literally, 'sent'. From this root we derive our words 'dismissed', 'commissioned' and 'mission'. We are commissioned, like the women at Jesus' empty tomb, who were told to go and tell what they had seen (Matthew 28:7).

Christ can be proclaimed through the way in which we live each moment. Fortunately, it does not all depend on us. If we are willing to be used by God, God will take us at our word, and often surprise us with the outcome.

We little realise what God could do in us if we abandoned ourselves totally to him and asked him to do in us whatever he wanted.

ST IGNATIUS LOYOLA (1491–1556)

A WORD FOR WEAVING:
Go in peace to love and serve the Lord.

63. TAKEN UP INTO CHRIST'S OFFERING

The Sending Out II

. . . we thank you for feeding us
with the body and blood of your Son Jesus Christ.
Through him we offer you our souls and bodies
to be a living sacrifice.

HOLY COMMUNION, ORDER ONE, *COMMON WORSHIP*

Strengthened by the Eucharist we now prepare to go and continue Christ's work in our daily lives.

This may prove costly.

You are to be taken,
blessed,
broken,
and given,
that the work of the incarnation may go on.

ST AUGUSTINE OF HIPPO (354–430)

Both St Peter and St Paul knew what it meant to find ourselves mysteriously linked with the suffering of Jesus:

But rejoice insofar as you are sharing Christ's sufferings,
so that you may also be glad and shout for joy when his
glory is revealed.

1 PETER 4:13

Now I rejoice in my sufferings for your sake, and in my
flesh I complete what is lacking in Christ's afflictions for
the sake of his body . . .

ST PAUL IN COLOSSIANS 1:24 (RSV)

We have received the cup of life, the wellspring of joy. Now Jesus invites us to take up our cross, and experience both the challenge and the fulfilment of following him.

Take my life, Lord;
guide me into the truth of who I am.

Teach me to recognise the promptings of your Spirit,
the intimations of joy,
the desire to serve you
that springs from the deepest places of my heart.

Give me the courage and strength I need
to accept the cost of following you,
and help me to deal generously and wisely
with any difficulties or conflicts
that may come my way.

A Word for Weaving:
Take my life, Lord.

64. A EUCHARISTIC WAY OF LIFE

The Sending Out III

From the Liturgy, and especially from the Eucharist, grace flows out into us as from a fountain.
CONSTITUTION ON THE SACRED LITURGY
(SECOND VATICAN COUNCIL) 1:10.

*Lord, teach us to live out
the meaning and message of Eucharist
in everything we do.*

May we embrace with thankfulness the gift of life.

May we recognise your presence in and through all things.

*May we handle created things reverently,
        paying attention to the earth and its seasons,
        sharing and eating meals with grateful hearts,
        valuing each person, and using each place well,
        so that everything is consecrated to you.*

*May we who have shared your cup be a household of thanksgiving,
        celebrating your abundant goodness,
        weaving our life into the liturgy
        and our liturgy into life,
        as we join our praise with the songs of the angels:*

'Heaven and earth are full of your glory!'

*Your gift of Eucharist shows us
the sublime in the ordinary, the mystery in the meal.*

153

Make all of our lives into a sign of your presence,
and guide us into ways of being
and patterns of praying
that draw us ever closer to you
in the dance of trust and love that is faith.

Holy, holy, holy God,
we pray as pilgrims in your temple,
dancing in the mystery of your encircling love,
and finding everywhere is holy ground.

GRAHAM KEYES

A WORD FOR WEAVING:
Heaven and earth are full of your glory!

EPILOGUE – THE WINE STILL DANCES

Dance then, wherever you may be,

I am the Lord of the Dance, said he,

And I'll lead you all wherever you may be,

And I'll lead you all in the Dance, said he.

SYDNEY CARTER

You can't keep Jesus down!

His unquenchable and irrepressible life inspires us still, as he invites us to take the risk of sharing in the feast of fools and joining the dance of love, which is the dance of God.

We are gifted with whatever of himself God has chosen to share with us

There is so much to celebrate, because we are – incredibly – invited to be friends of Jesus and join in God's ongoing work of creating and redeeming the world.

All that God asks of us is our consent.

Even our capacity to say Yes has been placed in us by God.

Everything is gift! Everything is grace!

Let them praise his name with dancing!   PSALM 149:3A

POST SCRIPT

A EUCHARISTIC VISION OF LIFE

More thankfulness, less complaining.

More awareness, less distraction.

More delight, less duty.

More receiving, less striving.

More healing rituals, less mindless rushing.

More going with life's rhythms, less fighting the tide of time.

More reverencing God's creation – less careless use of it.

More openness, less defensiveness.

More generosity, less judging.

More trust in God, less relying on myself.

> More belonging, more sharing;
> More Christ in me, more my true self;
> More wine, more dancing!

Some Final Questions

In calling us to share our lives with him, Christ does not lead us into ready-made answers, but into questions that will not go away.

In spite of low church-attendance in the West, we are a spiritually hungry generation. The way we craft, manage and engage with our worship can feed or starve our inner hunger for God.

• How much attention do we give to beauty and colour, music and atmosphere, symbolism and silence, alongside our necessary concern with words?

• To what extent do we tap the creative, prayerful and imaginative gifts of our congregations in our planning and preparing of services?

• What messages do we give by the way we arrange our furniture and use the physical space in our churches?

• How is the language in our worship understood and interpreted by our visitors and by those who are uncertain about faith? What is our best response to this?

• How attentively do we pray our worship?

• How much of ourselves do we open up to God when we worship?

NOTES AND ACKNOWLEDGEMENTS

When a quotation from the Bible starts in the middle of a sentence in the original translation, I have changed the first letter to a capital, and omitted the three dots that would normally mark a point in mid-sentence in the source. This applies in Sections 1, 5 (two quotes), 7, 9, 20, 27 (two quotes), 32, 35, 36 (A Word for Weaving), 40, 43 (final quote) and 61.

The word 'he' in the original has been replaced by the name 'Jesus' where the sense requires it, in Sections 1, 8 and 59.

Prologue
Buzz Aldrin's description of the wine swirling up the chalice is in *Men from Earth*, Buzz Aldrin and Malcolm McConnell, (New York: Bantam Books, 1989), pp.239–240.

Introduction
1. From the Greek verb *epi-phanein*, to reveal or make manifest.
2. The Holy Communion Service in *The Book of Common Prayer*, and its most commonly used form, as found in Order Two, *Common Worship* (pp. 229ff.), follow a different sequence.

PART 1.
1. The Victory of Love
For the sake of clarity, the word 'he' has been replaced by the name 'Jesus' in the initial quotation from Luke 22.

2. The Dance of Love
'The glory of God . . .': quote from Michael Ramsey: I have not been able to trace the exact source of this quotation. Ramsey discusses the glory of God as seen in St John's account of the self-giving love and Passion of Jesus in *Jesus and the Living Past* (Oxford University Press, 1980), pp.46–7 and 70–1.

A Word for Weaving is based on Jesus' 'new commandment' given to the disciples after he had washed their feet, John 13:34.

3. Could He have Given More?
Words from Julian of Norwich: paraphrase of lines taken from Chapter 22 of *A Lesson of Love: The Revelations of Divine Love* by

Julian of Norwich, edited and translated by Father John-Julian OJN (London, DLT, 1988), p.51.

5. **You in Me, I in You**
'Abide in me and I in you': cf. John 15:4.

Words of St Augustine: *Confessions,* Book VII, translated by R.S. Pine-Coffin (Harmondsworth: Penguin, 1961), p.147.

6. **Uncontainable Generosity**
'He always loved those . . .': From Eucharistic Prayer IV, *The Sunday Missal* (London: CollinsLiturgical, 1997), p.53.

'The "eye for an eye" kind of justice': in the Sermon on the Mount Jesus challenges the Old Testament edict of 'an eye for an eye' (cf. Leviticus 24:20), and teaches that we should love our enemies (cf. Matthew 5:38–48).

7. **He Needs Us**
'He leans his head on my shoulder': this imaginative detail is inspired by the painting *The Washing of Feet* by Sieger Köder, ©1997 St Paul Multimedia Productions.

Verse by Charles Péguy: the original is in *Oevres Poétiques Completes* (Paris: Gallimard. Bibliothéque de la Pléiade, 1954):
Il s'est mis dans le cas d'avoir besoin de nous.
Quelle imprudence. Quelle confiance.
Bien, mal placée, cela depend de nous.
Quelle espérance, quelle opiniâtreté, quel partis-pris,
quelle force incurable d'espérance.
En nous.
Translation from *The Holy Innocents and Other Poems,* Pansy Pakenham, Harvill Press, 1956

8. **The Passover Journey**
For the sake of clarity, the word 'he' has been replaced by the name 'Jesus' in the initial quotation from Luke 22.

We cannot be certain whether the Last Supper was a Passover meal, because the Gospels disagree. According to Mark (14:12) and Luke (22:7) the Passover lamb was sacrificed on the same day as the Last Supper, making this the Passover meal which Jesus 'desired to eat' with the disciples (Luke 22:15). Matthew agrees (26:17). But John says that Jesus died on the day of preparation (18:28, 19:14), making the Last Supper an eve-of-Passover meal. By this timing, Jesus died at the moment the Passover lambs were sacrificed, with a symbolism that is obviously powerful. The actions of Jesus at the meal could have applied to an ordinary meal as much as to the Passover. Either way, the Passover overtones of the meal are undeniable.

The Passover was originally a semi-nomadic spring festival, in which divine protection was invoked for shepherds moving out of the safety of winter pastures into the hazards of new territories. The Israelites inherited and adapted this, and took over several rituals from the original pagan festival, such as the roasted animal, unleavened bread, bitter herbs, belts fastened, and blood smeared on tent poles or door frames for protection.

'Christ the Bread of Life': cf. John 6:35.

'Jesus the Way, the Truth and the Life': cf. John 14:6.

Verses by Joyce Rupp: *in Dear Heart, Come Home* (New York: Crossroad, 1998), p.103.

10. **Holy Fire**
Gregory of Nyssa: cf. *On the Life of Moses* 401, sections A–D, quoted in *The Holy Fire* (New York: St Vladimir's Seminary Press, 1980) pp.155–6.

'Moses entered the cloud and came close to the ineffable, divine glory . . .': see also Exodus 19:16-25 and Exodus 33:18-23.

'Pour upon the poverty of our love . . .': Supplementary Texts at the Preparation of the Table, No. 12, *Common Worship* (London: Church House Publishing, 2000), p. 293.

12. **The New Covenant – God's Promise**
The word 'new' in the quotation from Matthew 26 appears in a

footnote in the NRSV, as occurring in 'other ancient authorities'.

Other covenants between God and his people in the Old Testament include one with Noah in Genesis 9:13, and with Abraham in Genesis 15:18–21 and 17:4–14, cf. also the 'new covenant' proclaimed by Jeremiah (31:31–34).

'Though we rejected your love . . .': *The Methodist Worship Book,* (Peterborough, The Methodist Publishing House, 1999), p.124.

13. The Vine
Wine is seen as a symbol of abundance and well-being in Amos 9:13–14. But in Old Testament teaching, when Israel is unfaithful, the vines deteriorate because of pests (Deuteronomy 28:39) or the ravaging of enemies (Psalm 80:8–18).

shalom: a Hebrew word, often translated 'peace', but with a wide spectrum of meanings, including 'well-being', 'prosperity', and 'harmony'.

Quote from *The Didache* 9,2: in *Prayers of the Eucharist: Early and Reformed,* 3rd edition (New York: Pueblo Publishing Company, 1987), p.23. *The Didache* includes many prayers with a clear Jewish origin, and this text is likely to be a reference to a Eucharistic meal.

14. Going to our Head
'Pressed down, shaken together, running over': echoing Luke 6:38a.

'We can let it go to our head': I owe this idea to the Revd Dagmar Winter.

Quote from Hildegard of Bingen: *Scivias, 2. V6, 21.* Translated by Hozeski (New Mexico: Bear & Co, 1986), p.143.

16. Jesus' Sacrifice
Much of this section is inspired by the teaching of Fr Kevin Seasoltz OSB.

The Latin noun *sacrifacium* is derived from *sacer facere*, 'to make or do something holy'.

Jesus' challenge to legalistic religion: e.g. Matthew 23:13ff. Luke 11:38–54.

A Word for Weaving is from the hymn *When I survey the wondrous cross*, by Isaac Watts (1674–1748), in *Hymns Ancient & Modern Revised*, London, Clowes and Sons Ltd, No.108.

17. Links across Time and Space

koinonia is a Greek word for 'fellowship', and occurs in the original Greek New Testament, for example, in 2 Corinthians 13:14 and Philippians 1:5.

'All the communions of a life-time . . .': Pierre Teilhard de Chardin, *Le Milieu Divine*, (English Translation, London: Fontana, 1962), p.124.

'From age to age you gather a people . . .': from Eucharistic Prayer III, *The Sunday Missal* (London: CollinsLiturgical, 1997), p.48.

A Word for Weaving is from *Common Worship*, Holy Communion, Order One, p.179.

18. A Glimpse of Heaven

'If there is a journey . . .': from the song *The Best is Still to Come* by Tom McGuiness, on the tape *All Will be Well*, X-4702, McCrimmon Publishing Co Ltd.

A Word for Weaving, 'Christ has died . . .': in Eucharistic Prayers A, B, C, E and G, in Order One of Holy Communion, *Common Worship*.

PART 2.

Next to the title page:

'Who would know Sinne . . .': George Herbert, *The Agonie*, in *The English Poems of George Herbert*, edited by C.A. Patrides (London: Dent, 1974). The last two lines are quoted again in Section 19.

22. Jesus Becomes the Cup

'Emptying himself of all but love . . .' *The Methodist Worship Book,* (Peterborough, The Methodist Publishing House, 1999), p. 137.

'the *fiat* of his mother . . .': *fiat* is the Latin for 'let it be', and refers to Mary's 'Yes' to the angel Gabriel at the Annunciation (Luke 1:38). I owe to Anne Lepine the idea of linking the *fiat* of Mary to that of Jesus.

'And a sword pierced both their hearts': cf. Simeon's words to Mary, 'a sword will pierce your own soul too.' (Luke 2:35)

23. Unstoppable Power

A Word for Weaving: The words, 'Behold the man!' were spoken by Pilate when Jesus was brought out, having been scourged, to stand before the crowds (John 19:5, RSV).

24. Judas

'Do quickly what you have to do.': John 13:27, NEB.
'whom he still calls "Friend?"': cf. Matthew 26:50.
'Woe to the one . . .': Matthew 26:24b.
'lost and feel destroyed by what we have done': cf. John 17:12, where Judas is referred to as 'the one destined to be lost' or 'the son of destruction' (footnote, NRSV).
'whose compassion reaches beyond the heavens . . .': cf. Psalm 103:11.

25. Every Time Someone Cries in Pain

'Even though I walk through the valley of the shadow of death . . .': from the New Revised Standard Version, but using the alternative translation as given in the footnote.

Quote by Maria Boulding: *The Coming of God,* (London: SPCK, 1982), p.135.

26. The Brokenness of the World

Passage from St John Chrysostom: *Homily on St Matthew,* No. 50, paragraph 3. Quoted in Thomas Merton, *The Living Bread,* (Tunbridge Wells: Burns & Oates, 1956), pp.109–10.

28. 'Can you Drink this Cup?'
Quote from John Hadley, *Bread of the World*, (London: Darton Longman & Todd, 1989), p. 93.

'To set the earth ablaze . . .' is © 1997 International Commission on English in the Liturgy, Inc. It is from the Collect for the Nineteenth Sunday in Ordinary Time, Year C, *Opening Prayers – The ICEL Collects* (Norwich: The Canterbury Press, 1997), p.95. Reproduced with permission.

PART 3.
30. The Potter
Verses by Joyce Rupp: *The Cup of Our Life* (Indiana: Ave Maria Press, 1997), p.90.

31. God Needs Empty Vessels
'Come to this sacred table . . .' *The Methodist Worship Book*, p.158.
'Behold, Lord, an empty vessel . . .': prayer of Martin Luther. In *The Oxford Book of Prayer*, edited by George Appleton (Oxford University Press, 1985), No.137.

32. Unprotected Love
I owe the idea of prayer as 'unprotected love' to Fr Simon Holden CR.
'In the foolishness of the divine love . . .': cf. 1 Corinthians 1:25; 3:18–19; 4:10–13.

33. The Wound of Love
Verse by Hildegard of Bingen: *Scivias, 3. V10.7*. Translated by Hozeski (New Mexico: Bear & Co, 1986), p.329.

34. Learning to Receive
Prayer beginning 'O Holy Spirit . . .': exact source unknown, although it has been rather vaguely attributed to 'the late Bishop of Bloemfontein'. In *The Book of a Thousand Prayers*, edited by Angela Ashwin (London: HarperCollins, 1996), No.44.

36. The Cup of Thanksgiving
Quote by Frances Young: in the essay *The Great Thanksgiving Prayer*, in *Living the Eucharist*, edited by Stephen Conway

(London: Darton, Longman & Todd, 2001), p.86.

37. Bodily Worship
Prayer from the Malabar Liturgy; exact source unknown.

38. Co-Creators with God
Worship as a 'corporate creative activity' is a phrase from the late Michael Vasey.

Quote by Joseph A. Brown: *To Stand on the Rock: Meditations on Black Catholic Identity*, (Maryknoll, NY: Orbis Books, 1998), p.2.

'O worship the Lord . . .': (based on Psalm 29:2), first line of the hymn by J.S.B. Monsell (1811–75), in *Hymns Ancient & Modern Revised*, London, Clowes and Sons Ltd, No.77.

39. Fools for Christ
The woman who poured perfumed ointment over Jesus' head: Mark 14:3–9.

The phrase 'the foolishness of God' is in 1 Corinthians 1:25 (RSV).

On 'wasting time' in worship: cf. Marva Dawn's book about liturgy, *A Royal 'Waste' of Time*, (Grand Rapids, Michigan: William B. Eerdmans Publishing Company, 1999).

Quote from Romano Guardini: *The Spirit of the Liturgy* (New York: Crossroad Publishing Company, 1998 edition). Translated by Joanne M. Pierce, pp.68,70.

In the passage from Proverbs 8, the Hebrew word for 'master craftsman' is sometimes translated 'little child'.

Quote from John Drury: *Angels and Dirt* (London: Darton, Longman & Todd, 1972) p. 92.

40. Letting Go.
Prayer of St Ignatius, 'Take, Lord, as your right . . .': in *The Book of a Thousand Prayers*, edited by Angela Ashwin (London:

HarperCollins, 1996), No.27.

41. Listen!
On the subject of silence in worship, see also Part 4, Section 45, *Words Placed in Silence*.

Lines by Brendan Kennelly in: *A Time for Voices – Selected Poems 1960–1990*, (Newcastle upon Tyne: Bloodaxe Books, 1990), pp.101–2.

'In the silence and stillness . . .': *The Methodist Worship Book*, p.129.

PART 4.
Next to the title page:
'. . . he (Jesus) has shared our life, and he has transformed it.': I owe this insight to Bishop David Stancliffe, in a sermon delivered in Christchurch Cathedral, Dublin, on Trinity Sunday 2000, and in the essay *The Fraction and the Shape of the Rite*, in *Living the Eucharist*, edited by Stephen Conway, (London: Darton, Longman & Todd, 2001), p.95.

42. Formed into Community
The two opening greetings are from *Common Worship*, Holy Communion, Order One, page 167.

A Word for Weaving is based on Ephesians 4:3.

43. Our Forgiving God
Opening prayer: 'Most merciful God . . .': *Common Worship*, page 169.

'waits to welcome and embrace us': like the father of the prodigal son (Luke 15:11–24).

Kyrie eleison! is Greek for 'Lord have mercy'.

44. Glory to God!
Opening text: the words of the angels, 'peace, good will among people,' are from the New Revised Standard Version, but using the alternative translation as given in the footnote.

Quote from Annie Dillard, *Holy the Firm* (New York: Harper & Row, 1977), p.45.

45. Words Placed in Silence
On the subject of silence in worship, see also Part 3, Section 41, *Listen!*

'Almighty God, you have made us . . .': *Common Worship*, p.418. Based on a prayer by St Augustine of Hippo (354–430).

'Our worship needs moments of quietness . . .': an increasing number of churches are finding that moments of corporate silence, at appropriate points within the flow of the liturgy, can enrich worship. For example, *Common Worship*, Note 8 (p.331) suggests: 'Silence is particularly appropriate within the Prayers of Penitence and of Intercession, before the Collect, in response to the reading of the Scriptures, after the Eucharistic Prayer and after the distribution.'

The phrase 'mark, learn and inwardly digest': *Common Worship*, from the Collect for the Last Sunday after Trinity, p.494.

Quote from Aidan Kavanagh: *Elements of Rite* (Collegeville: The Liturgical Press, 1982), p.51.

'Let all mortal flesh . . .': *Hymns Ancient & Modern Revised*, London, Clowes and Sons Ltd, No.390, verse 1.

46. The Breaking of the Word
I owe several of the examples in this and the following section to John Hadley's book *Bread of the World* (London: Darton, Longman & Todd, 1989).

Liturgy of St John Chrysostom (Basilica of St Mary in Cosmedin, 1975). This text, with origins in the seventh century, (and which is probably has little to do with the fourth century saint John Chrysostom himself), is the liturgy most regularly used in Orthodox churches.

Quote from Romero Guardini: *Before Mass*, translated by E.C.

Briefs (London: Longmans, Green and Co, 1957), pp.11–12.

47. We Believe

The quote from Hilary of Poitiers is from *De Trinitate II:2*, cited by Maurice Wiles in *The Making of Christian Doctrine* (Cambridge 1967), pp.32ff.

48. Praying for Others

'In the power of the Spirit and in union with Christ . . .': *Common Worship*, Supplementary Texts, Forms of Intercession, pp.281–7.

Quote from Mother Mary Clare SLG: *Encountering the Depths* (London: Darton, Longman and Todd, 1981), p. 55.

'our small energy of desire . . .': cf. the prayer by Evelyn Underhill (1875–1941): 'Accept and transform my small energy of desire, that it may become part of your great energy of desire . . .'. In the *Book of a Thousand Prayers*, edited by Angela Ashwin (London: HarperCollins, 1996), No.401.

49. 'Peace be with you'

'The peace of the Lord be always with you . . .': *Common Worship*, Holy Communion, Order One, p.175.

The quote from a homily of St Augustine of Hippo (354–430) is in *Patrologica Latina* 38: pp.1246–8. Edited by J.-P. Migne. Translated by Nathan Mitchell.

A Word for Weaving echoes Jesus' prayer in John 17:11.

50. Offering our Ordinariness

'All things come from you, O Lord . . .': *Common Worship*, Prayers at the Preparation of the Table, p.291. I have added the words 'O Lord'.

51. Celebrating Creation

'Yours, Lord, is the greatness . . .': *Common Worship*, Prayers at the Preparation of the Table, p.291.

'And, behold, it is very good!': cf. Genesis 1:31a.

Reredos: translated by Cynthia and Saunders Davies, in the book they edited entitled, *Euros Bowen, Priest/Poet* (Church in Wales Publication, 1993), p.75.

52. With Delight we Join in this Prayer

The opening dialogue: *Common Worship*, all Eucharistic Prayers in Order One, pp.184–204. (I have divided the first stanza into two sentences when I quote it a second time.)

53. A Sacrifice of Thanksgiving

'You are worthy of our thanks and praise . . .': *Common Worship*, pp.198–9.

54. The Songs of the Angels

'As the Eastern churches teach us . . .': cf. Timothy Ware, *The Orthodox Church* (Harmondsworth: Penguin Books, 1967), Chapter 13: *Orthodox Worship I: The Earthly Heaven.*

'Therefore with angels and archangels . . .': *Common Worship*, pp.185, 188 and 191.

'And so, with all the faithful . . .': *The Methodist Worship Book*, p.180.

55. The Importance of the Meal

'On the night before he died . . .': *Common Worship*, p. 202.

'as "com-panions" – literally "bread-sharers" . . .': the word 'com-panions' comes from the Latin, *cum + panis*, meaning, literally 'with' + 'bread'.

56. 'We remember'

The New Testament Greek word for 'remembrance' is *anamnesis*. Scholars vary in their interpretations of this word. Cf. the article by W. Jardine Grisbrooke in *A New Dictionary of Liturgy & Worship*, edited by J G Davies, (London: SCM Press, 1986) p.18, in contrast to Paul Bradshaw, *Early Christian Worship* (London: SPCK, 1996), pp.45, 53–5.

57. Pentecost Continues

The petition, 'Send down your Spirit' is sometimes referred to as the *epiclesis*, which is the Greek word for 'invocation'. This is a specific calling down of the Holy Spirit upon the gifts or upon the worshippers, or both. It may come before or after the narrative of the Last Supper, and is sometimes found in both places (in a 'double epiclesis'). See *A Companion to Common Worship*, edited by Paul Bradshaw (London: SPCK, 2001), pp.126–7.

'Father, by your Holy Spirit . . .': Common Worship, p.199.

58. Our Whole-Hearted 'Yes!'
'Through Jesus Christ our Lord; by whom . . .': *Common Worship*, pp.190 and 193. The capital letters and exclamation mark are my own.

59. 'Abba, Father!'
For the sake of clarity, the word 'he' has been replaced by the name 'Jesus' in the initial quotation from Luke 11.

'the prayer can appropriately come at other moments . . .': in the prayer books of some provinces of the Anglican Communion, such as *A New Zealand Prayer Book*, an alternative position is given for the Lord's Prayer, at the end of the Intercessions. In three of the nine forms of Holy Communion in *The Methodist Worship Book* (1999), the Lord's Prayer comes only at the end of the Intercessions.

60. Broken Bread, People United
'Lamb of God . . .': *Common Worship*, Holy Communion, Order One, p.179.

'friends and companions . . .': 'com-panion' is from the Latin *cum* + *panis* (see note for Section 55).

61. The Gift
'and know your kingdom truly within me . . .': cf. the various versions of Luke 17:21, where the Greek word *entos* could be translated as 'among', 'in the midst of' or 'within'.

62. Go Out!

'Send us out in the power of your Spirit . . .': *Common Worship*, p.182.

'We little realise . . .': Exact source unknown. Quoted in a sermon by a member of staff at St Beuno's Ignatian Spirituality Centre, St Asaph, N. Wales, from the Fourth Week of the Spiritual Exercises of St Ignatius. Cf. *Draw me into your Friendship, A Literal Translation and A Contemporary Reading of The Spiritual Exercises*, David L. Fleming (Saint Louis, 1996).

63. Taken up into Christ's Offering
'We thank you for feeding us . . .': *Common Worship*, p.182.
'take up our cross . . .': cf. Matthew 16:24.

'You are to be taken. . .': quote from St Augustine, on a prayer card. Exact source unknown.

64. A Eucharistic Way of Life
Constitution on the Sacred Liturgy – Second Vatican Council, (London: Catholic Truth Society, 1967) 1:10.

'Weaving our life into the liturgy and our liturgy into life . . .': a variety of ways of praying at home can reflect what happens in church, e.g. using seasonal pictures or icons; making an Advent wreath; following a particular way of praying during Lent; using candles that were part of special services in church; incorporating words from the liturgy – including seasonal ones – into grace at meals, or into a daily office.

The word 'liturgy' (Greek: *leitourgia*) means, literally, 'the work of the people', and there is a healthy emphasis on worship as the work of the whole assembly in current thinking about worship and especially the Eucharist. In practice the word 'liturgy' is used in several ways, including 'set prayers' as opposed to spontaneous or 'free' prayer. In this book I use the word 'liturgy' to refer to public Eucharistic worship in its ecumenically agreed shape and form.

Prayer by Graham Keyes: in *The Book of a Thousand Prayers*, edited by Angela Ashwin (London: HarperCollins, 1996), No 868.

Epilogue: The Wine Still Dances

'Dance then, wherever you may be . . .': verse 1 of *Lord of the Dance*, © Sydney Carter, in *Faith, Folk and Clarity* (Great Yarmouth: Galliard, 1967), p.13.

In the final quotation from Psalm 149, the exclamation mark is my own.

Every effort has been made to trace sources and obtain permission for copyright material. I apologise if correction is needed, and will amend any reprint of this book if necessary.

ILLUSTRATIONS

Cover:	© Sophie Hacker
Prologue:	© Sister Anna SSM

*This picture is reproduced
in a smaller version on
page* 155 *(The Epilogue).*

Title page, Part 1 – page 23:	© Sister Theresa Margaret CHN
Title page, Part 2 – page 57:	© Cecil Collins, *The Agony in the Garden*, reproduced with permission from the estate of the late Elisabeth Collins.

*This picture is reproduced
in a smaller version on
page* 64 *(Section 22)*

Title page, Part 3 – page 79:	© Sister Theresa Margaret CHN
Title page, Part 4 – page 105:	© From *In the Light of Christ*, Vols 1–2, (Great Wakering: McCrimmons, 1998), No. LC337, p.119.

PATTERNS NOT PADLOCKS
Angela Ashwin

Do you ever feel frayed at the edges, stressed and generally pressurised, squeezed and harassed?

In *Patterns not Padlocks* Angela Ashwin interprets these experiences and gently suggests practical ideas and initiatives for prayer and spiritual vitality building on the chaotic busy-ness of everyday life rather than avoiding it. An accompanying cassette tape (available separately) contains a series of brief talks and meditations and music

I found this book inspiring and containing several helpful ideas on prayer.
EVANGELISM TODAY

Sustaining the habit of prayer in an exhausting life is difficult . . . this book is intended to help people who find difficulty discouraging. There are plenty of ideas on how to make the best of chaos.
THE CHURCH TIMES

Whatever your situation, there is much to be gleaned from this useful book. I heartily recommend it.
THE CHRISTIAN HERALD

0 86347 088 2 (book)
0 86347 279 6 (cassette tape)

WAIT AND SEE
WAIT AND TRUST

Angela Ashwin

Angela Ashwin aims to equip you to pray and
to meditate – putting down ever-deeper roots in
the stillness and quiet of God – however busy you
may be.

WAIT AND SEE and WAIT AND TRUST are pocket-sized
books that start with helpful introductions on simple
ways of finding time for prayer and getting the most
out of those times. The thematic meditations are
complimented by Bible verses and specially commissioned art and calligraphy that combine to help you
pray with your eyes and intuition as well as with your
mind and reason.

*With lovely water colour pictures and simple yet very
clear comments from Scripture and with some of the
author's own ideas, we are drawn closer into the
presence of the Lord. This will help your prayer life and
your spiritual growth!*
DIRECTIONS

WAIT AND SEE (0 86347 207 9)
WAIT AMD TRUST (0 86347 208 7)